**BRENT LIBRARIES**
Please return/renew this item
by the last date shown.
Books may also be renewed by
phone or online.
Tel: 0115 929 3388
On-line **www.brent.gov.uk/libraryservice**

Some other titles from How to Books

**How to Research Your House**
*Everyone tells a story...*

**@ Home with Your Ancestors.com**
*How to research family history using the internet*

**Times of Our Lives**
*The essential companion for writing your own life story*

**Tracking Down Your Ancestors**
*Discover the story behind your ancestors and bring your family history to life*

**The Beginner's Guide to Tracing Your Roots**
*An inspirational and encouraging introduction to discovering your family's past*

**howto**books
Please send for a free copy of the latest catalogue:

How To Books
Spring Hill House, Spring Hill Road
Begbroke, Oxford OX5 1RX, United Kingdom
Tel: (01865) 375794. Fax: (01865) 379162.
info@howtobooks.co.uk
www.howtobooks.co.uk

# HOW TO
# RESEARCH
# LOCAL
# HISTORY

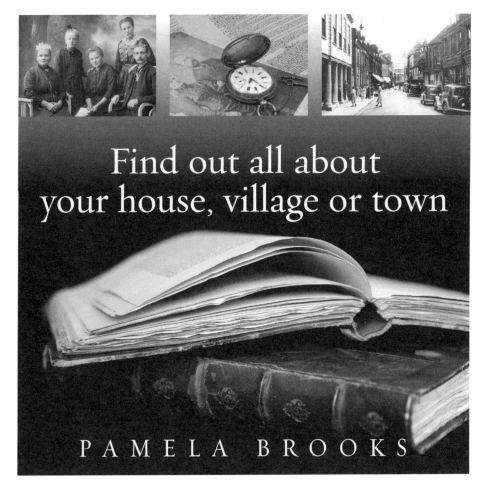

## Find out all about
## your house, village or town

### PAMELA BROOKS

**howto**books

Published by How To Books Ltd
Spring Hill House, Spring Hill Road,
Begbroke, Oxford OX5 1RX
Tel: (01865) 375794. Fax: (01865) 379162
info@howtobooks.co.uk
www.howtobooks.co.uk

First published 2006
Second edition 2008

© Pamela Brooks 2008

British Library Cataloguing in Publication Data
A catalogue record for this book is available from the British Library

ISBN: 978 1 84528 276 9

Cover design by Baseline Arts Ltd, Oxford
Produced for How to Books by Deer Park Productions, Tavistock
Typeset by Pantek Arts Ltd, Maidstone, Kent
Printed and bound by Cromwell Press Ltd, Trowbridge, Wiltshire

# Contents

For Gerard, Christopher and Chloë, with all my love

# Preface

I am delighted to have updated *How To Research Local History* for its second edition.

As with the first edition, the book is aimed at people who are new to researching local history – people who are interested in knowing where they come from and what happened in their area – and the book retains its practical, no-nonsense nature.

Some of the entries have been expanded (particularly the section on maps). There are also two new appendices: one is a simplified guide to pre-Decimal weights and measures, and the other is a glossary of common terms found when working with old documents, for quick reference. I have also expanded the index to make it easier for you to find the information you need.

*Pamela Brooks*

$$\left( 1 \right)$$

# Introduction

---

This chapter covers the definition of local history and reasons why you might want to study it, and gives an outline of the different types of historical evidence.

## LOOKING AT WHAT LOCAL HISTORY IS

Local history is about the people, places, institutions and communities in your area; it is a way of building up a picture of what your town or city looked like in the past, who lived there and what they did. Sometimes local events will have national importance, such as civil war battles; sometimes they might seem unimportant to someone on the other side of the country, but had a big impact in your local area (such as fires or floods).

Local history is all about looking at the facts, analysing what those facts tell us, and comparing it with what was happening nationally at the time. You may find yourself switching between different sources so you can build up the picture of the past – you're unlikely to find all the information you want in one place. So many of the records mentioned in Chapter 3, for example, would shed light on buildings and institutions as well as people, and the records mentioned in Chapter 4 would shed light on people as well as the places they lived, worked, spent leisure time and prayed.

But do bear in mind it's not always possible to find out the whole story about what happened, because the source material might be limited or even missing.

## LOOKING AT REASONS TO STUDY LOCAL HISTORY

History is becoming more and more popular. People are fascinated with their own family past and enjoy finding out more about their ancestors; and that can often shift into an interest in wanting to know more about *where* they come from as well as who! You might have moved into an old house and want to know who lived there before you. You might have seen an article about your street or village and want to know more about what happened there in the past. You might have seen an article in the local newspaper about a local famous person and want to know more about them. Or you might be interested in a theme, such as an industry, domestic service, public health, schools, the workhouse or local pubs.

You might want to study local history just for your own interest – but it's worth bearing in mind that local magazines and newspapers might be interested in your findings. Whether it's the parish magazine, the local glossy magazine or even the Saturday supplement of your local paper, it's worth sharing what you find because other people might be asking the same questions – and might have answers you haven't found yet.

You don't have to be a trained historian to be interested in and research local history; all you need is an interest, an enquiring mind, an ability to keep your notes in an order where you can retrieve information quickly, and perseverance to follow a trail. Though if you want to take a formal course in local history, you could try your local university. Ask at your local library – they will have details of evening classes and possibly courses run by the Workers' Educational Association (WEA). Some libraries and associations (such as the Oral History Society) run courses on particular topics, such as using a census, tracing a house's history and how to record and structure interviews.

## LOOKING AT DIFFERENT TYPES OF HISTORICAL EVIDENCE

Historical evidence falls into several categories:

◆ Primary
◆ Secondary
◆ Oral
◆ Physical

Below is a quick guide to what you can expect to find in each category; they are covered in more detail further on in the book. It's also worth noting that one source might be useful for different things – for example, title deeds can tell you about a building and about its occupants, as can street directories and maps (particularly those with schedules such as the tithe awards).

### Defining primary evidence

Primary evidence tends to be written, and are original manuscripts (though you may need to use microfilmed or microfiche versions for heavily used sources, which protects the original). These include:

◆ Records (legal documents such as title deeds and wills; parish registers; institution records such as school log books or hospital or prison registers; minutes and court books; industrial records, such as railway timetables and accident books)
◆ Handbills (advertisements, printed on a page or in a leaflet, which could publicise an event or a film, cinema, or exhibition)
◆ Diaries
◆ Letters
◆ Local collections, for example, theatre programmes or football club programmes.

*Looking at availability*

Scotland's administrative and legal systems aren't the same as those in England and Wales. Since the Middle Ages, English counties have had the same administrative systems; since the time of Henry VIII, Wales has used the same administrative systems as England.

Some counties have more records available than others; the southern English counties tend to have the best-preserved records, whereas the north and west are patchier. It also depends on how often records have been moved about, or if there has been any damage by fire or flood or enemy action during wartime.

*Looking at the Domesday Book*

The Domesday Book is another good starting point for background of the area you are researching. William the Conqueror ordered a very detailed survey of landowners' assets (including the Crown) and their liability to pay tax. It is known as the Domesday Book because it could not be appealed against. It was completed in 1086 and it is the first written record of many towns and villages. It lists the holders of lands within the county, then goes through each 'hundred' (the administrative district within the county) and lists details such as churches, fields, and houses.

For example, the entry for Norwich even states which houses are ruined and which are empty. Sometimes the owners and their occupations are listed, which can help you build up a picture of the community: for example, in Norwich Hundred, there are references to Hildebrand the lorimer (spurmaker), Gerard the watchman and Rabel the artificer among many others. 'Little Domesday' covers Norfolk, Suffolk and Essex; 'Great Domesday' deals with the rest of England (excluding London, Northumberland, Cumberland, Durham, Northern Westmoreland and Winchester).

## Defining secondary evidence

Secondary sources are very broad and often a good place to start when you are researching local history, because someone may already have written about the subject you want to know more about – there's no point in reinventing the wheel! However, perspectives and the way history is interpreted both change over the years, and new evidence can come to light, so you may be able to research a story better than a previous author. The best place to start is in the local studies section of your library. If your local library doesn't have the information you want, the librarians will be able to tell you if it's available in a different branch, the local record office or in a specialist archive.

Secondary sources include books, articles (contemporary and retrospective), biographies, and published letters. They may be based on original documents but they may contain errors or the author's personal bias, so it is often worth going back to the primary sources as well. Be particularly careful about transcriptions because it is very easy to misinterpret handwriting or abbreviations. Published works often have references to the original documents or other secondary sources which you might find helpful.

In 1586, William Camden produced *Britannia*, which is a description of every county. It was written in Latin, but was translated and enlarged in later years; Edmund Gibson produced a new edition in 1695, and Richard Gough produced two more editions in 1789 and 1806.

### Looking at county histories

County histories have been written by gentlemen scholars since around the 1660s, although one of the earliest extant county histories is William Lambarde's *Kent* (1576). In Norfolk, for example, there are eleven volumes of Blomefield's history and topography of the county. Other counties have standard histories, too, and the local studies department in your local library should have copies available or be able to tell you where to find them. It is also possible to buy copies in second-hand and antiquarian bookshops, though these can be prohibitively expensive; the last time I found a copy of Blomefield, the set was priced at over £3,000! You may be able to find some rare texts available as digitised versions on CD-Rom, so it is worth checking suppliers of archive CD material.

County histories tend to include:

- A general description of the county, its geology (rivers, hills, gorges, forests, natural features), its natural history (flora and fauna), and administration system.
- Lists of markets and fairs (usually in calendar order within each town).
- 'Political history' from Anglo-Saxon times to the present (this is where you need to be careful; the author's political sympathy might colour his or her view).
- Descriptions of each parish, arranged by 'hundred' (i.e. the county subdivisions). These include information about the manors within the parish, who owned them (often going back to the time of William the Conqueror), and churches and their monuments (some of which might no longer exist, so it is useful to know what was there), as well as important buildings.

County histories may also give information about events such as fires, floods, major trials and executions.

*Looking at the Victoria County History*

There is also the 'Victoria History of the Counties of England' (VCH for short), which covers most counties. The series started in 1899 and was dedicated to Queen Victoria. The volumes are usually found in the 'outsize volume' section and have a red cover. They have general sections which include prehistory, economic history and the history of the churches and chapels. They also have topographical sections which deal with the cities, towns and villages within the county, including buildings such as almshouses, manor houses and other important buildings. The VCH usually includes the text of the Domesday Book, as well as accounts of schools, religious houses and charities, and is a good starting point if you are looking at the history of a particular village.

*Looking at travellers' tales*
A description of the area can also be found in the notebooks of people who travelled around the country – for example, the *Journey of Celia Fiennes 1682–1706* and Defoe's *A Tour through the Whole Island of Great Britain*. Texts of both these books are available online at *www.visionofbritain.org.uk* – a searchable site which includes the complete texts of books describing journeys around Britain written between the 12th and 19th centuries. If you type in 'Norwich', for example, there are references to Defoe and Fiennes as above, as well as letters from William Cobbett and Charles Wesley and a tour by Arthur Young.

*Looking at works of antiquarians*
Many antiquarian societies were founded in the late 1800s; most of them produced journals which contain useful source material. Some antiquarians may also have compiled indexes of material (e.g. of local newspapers) which will save you time in researching.

Some antiquarians also made scrapbooks, collecting information on particular subjects. These are absolute goldmines and can contain anything from contemporary newspaper cuttings through to photographs, postcards, original documents, autographs and the like. You may come across them at antiques and collector's fairs, but you are more likely to find them in your local studies library.

*Looking at Local Record Societies*

Local Record Societies exist in most counties, and they tend to produce two sorts of material:

- Edited transcripts – these are transcripts of original documents. Some may be parallel translations of Latin or medieval records (i.e. showing the original and a modern English version), and most have an introductory chapter explaining more about the documents.
- Guide volumes – these are lists of types of documents (such as maps) or sources for subjects (such as enclosure).

## Defining oral evidence

The Oral History Society defines oral history as the recording of people's memories. They see it as filling in the gaps and include everyone's life stories ('everyone' means people whose views weren't normally included: the poor, women, people who were disabled, and those whose views were ignored because of their race or religion). Oral history can be recorded on audio or video tape; it includes recollections of national events as well as everyday events. Oral history is covered in more depth in Chapter 10.

## Defining physical evidence

Physical history takes several forms:

- The place itself – particularly in the case of buildings or street history
- Maps (see Chapter 7 for more details)
- Photographs, postcards and drawings – it's particularly interesting to compare drawings of buildings or street scenes from the early 20th century and the actual place as it is now
- Aerial photography – different coloured soils can identify features, such as a filled-in ditch which appears darker as the soil is wetter; a former settlement, which appears as a dark patch; or a Roman road,

which might appear as a wide pale stripe. Grass tends to look darker on the line of ditches and pale or yellow on the remains of buried walls. However, a lot depends on the light in which the photographs are taken, the angle of photography and the kind of cover on the ground, so you may need an archaeologist's help to interpret aerial photographs.

The study of local history can be deeply absorbing, so you may find yourself spending rather more time than you had anticipated among record sources. My family know from experience that if they go shopping while I spend a couple of hours in the local studies department, and they agree to meet me at a certain point and a certain time, they'll have to come and find me because I've lost track of the time!

$\left(\begin{array}{c}2\end{array}\right)$

# Preparing to Research

This chapter covers how to keep records of your information, how to prepare for visiting archives, practical tips on working with documents, and how to avoid the common pitfalls.

## KEEPING RECORDS

Organising your notes properly right from the start will save you a lot of time. If you just write everything down in a bound notebook, you won't risk losing anything – but you will also have to spend ages finding it again! So, before you start working, you need to think about the information you are collecting, how you want to use it, and the best way of retrieving the information quickly.

### Using a ring-binder (longhand)

As you make more notes on your subject, you'll find that they fall under different topics. For example, when I was researching *Norwich: Street by Street*, I knew that I wanted to cover the derivation of the street name, who lived there, events that happened on the streets, buildings of special interest and 'miscellaneous' – so I kept my notes in five sections right from the start.

The easiest way to make your notes (in longhand) is on A4 paper – then you can keep the separate sheets in a ring-binder, with subject dividers between the separate topics.

### Using a card index

A card index – where each piece of information is stored on a separate card, sorted by subject, within a box – is useful for finding information quickly, but as your research grows you may find yourself having to lug several enormous boxes around with you. Because the cards are stored 'loose' rather than clipped into a file, it is also easier to lose them or accidentally slip them into the wrong place.

## Using a computer

You may find it easier to type your notes straight onto computer. You may have a laptop; or your local library may have computer terminals available that you can use, though you will need some form of portable digital media with you (such as a flash drive) to store the file (or email it to your own mailbox). You may decide to keep your notes in longhand and type them up; that's fine, but keep your original notes as it's easy to make a typographical error, particularly on dates and the spellings of names, and you may need to refer back to your original notes.

Your notes can be stored in the same way as they would in a ring-binder. Each sheet of A4 is equivalent to a separate word-processing document, stored within a folder (equivalent to a subject divider) within your word-processing program. For example, if you are using Microsoft® Word, you can set up a directory within 'My Documents' for your research – let's call it NORWICH. Within that directory, you will have subdirectories (folders) for each bit of your research. For example, you might have files such as BUILDINGS or PEOPLE or EVENTS or TRANSPORT, as well as SOURCES (so you have an ongoing index of your sources and where to find them). Within the BUILDINGS directory, you might have files on pubs, churches, schools, civic buildings, private houses, and shops – whatever suits your need.

### Databases and spreadsheets

Databases and spreadsheets work in the same way as card index. With a database, you will need to decide what fields you need before you start researching (so make sure you use a flexible program that will allow you to add fields to your records as you need them). You will also need some mechanism to make sure records aren't duplicated or overwritten by mistake.

The advantages of using a computer include:

- You're less likely to make transcribing errors – it's easy to misread your longhand notes when typing them up, or to forget what you meant by an abbreviation, days or even weeks after you wrote your original notes
- You can search the files quickly for a relevant keyword (e.g. 'murder' or 'fire' or 'marriage')
- It's easy to insert and remove material (e.g. when listing sources alphabetically by author name) without making your notes messy
- If you're planning a book or article, you can cut and paste from your notes rather than having to retype it all.

However, there are disadvantages you need to plan round:

- The library or archive may not have a computer terminal available (you may need to book it in advance, and there may be a limit on how long you can use it)
- If you use a laptop, the library or archive may need a certificate from an approved electrician before you can use it on mains; if you are using battery power, be aware of how long the battery lasts before it needs recharging
- You need to keep a regular (*at least* weekly) back up of your files in case there's a problem with your computer and you lose data. It is best to use a CD-rom or a thumb drive (flash drive) for your main back up. It is also a good idea to keep two copies of a back up, because data can corrupt. Or keep a copy on a server – most internet service providers give you web space or access to a digital vault as

well as email addresses, and you can password-protect it so nobody can access your data without your permission

♦ It is easy to mistype information when transcribing, so if you are working straight to computer always double-check each paragraph to save yourself time in the future.

## Using computer tables

One of the simplest ways of making a database is to use a table in your word-processing program. For example, when I was researching *Norwich: Street by Street*, I set up a notes file for events within the city. My table had four columns: date, name, street name and event details. From newspaper reports, I knew when the event happened, where it happened, who was involved, and what the event was. My notes file looked something like this:

| Date | Name | Street | Event |
|------|------|--------|-------|
| 23.05.1801 | Weston, Charles | Upper Market Place (no 5) | Banker, won £15,000 in Irish Lottery |
| 9.11.1808 | Hudson, Mary | Gaol Hill | Escaped successfully from city gaol |
| 22.08.1832 | Atkins' Menagerie | Castle Ditches | First exhibition with a lion tamer |
| 01.08.1842 | Alleni | Ber Street | Accident in 'chariot of fire' at Greyhound Gardens |

I was working chronologically through the newspapers, so it was logical to put the table in date order. But by using a table in Word, I could reorder the information in alphabetical order by name of person or by street name (so I didn't have to search through the table to find which events happened on which street). A small amendment to the fourth column (e.g. adding Fire, Murder, Leisure or another heading as the first word of the entry in that cell) meant that I could also order my data by type of event. This was very useful when I started researching *The Norfolk Almanac of Disasters*, as I was able to pick out the fires, floods and extreme weather conditions, and had the bare bones of the story as well as the source (I had noted which newspaper contained the story), so I was able to go back and fill in more details.

In Word, to rearrange your table, you simply select the entire table, choose 'sort' from the Table menu and then choose which column you want to sort by. This approach also works well for a spreadsheet or database (but make sure your spreadsheet or database is compatible with your word-processing program, or you will end up duplicating effort).

## Noting your sources

It is important to make a note of your sources because:

- You may need to refer to thc source again later (and if you've noted it properly it will save you time locating the information again)
- If you are publishing your research as an article or book, you need to list your sources either as footnotes or in a bibliography.

The accepted way to list your sources is:

- Books – A.N. Author, *Title of Book* (publication date), place of publication, publisher, page number
- Articles – A.N. Author, 'Title of Article', *Title of Magazine*, volume number, issue number, (publication date), pages where the article appears
- Reports – A N author, *Title of Report* (publication date), name of organisation issuing the report, Report Number
- Internet articles: A.N. Author, (date), 'Title of Article', *Title of Online Magazine [Online]*, volume number, issue number, available from [URL reference, i.e. in the form http://website.co.uk/page-name.html], (date accessed)

◆ Other internet documents: A.N. Author, (date, if given), *Title of Document [Online]*, available from [URL reference, i.e. in the form http://website.co.uk/pagename.html], (date accessed).

Your local record office will be able to give you information about how to record the sources for original documents – for example, the tithe map and apportionment for Attleborough in Norfolk would be recorded as Norfolk Record Office (or NRO) DN/TA 84 (which stands for Diocese of Norwich/Tithe Apportionment). Most record offices have a system of letters (which identify the type of record) and numbers which they use to locate documents.

### Using quotes and keeping within the law

If you are quoting directly from your source, bear in mind the laws of copyright. If you quote more than 400 words from a book or 40 lines from a poem without permission from the copyright holder, you are infringing copyright and the copyright holder can take legal action against you. Copyright exists until 70 years after an author's death or (in the case of letters) 70 years after first publication; if you're not sure whether something is copyright or not, ask advice from staff at the archive base where you're looking at documents. The Society of Authors also has useful information on copyright.

To get permission to quote, you need to contact the rights department of the publisher and explain what you want to use, where you want to use it, and (if published) the copyright owner will want to know the print run and likely distribution of your work. You may need to pay a fee for using the quote (see also maps in chapter 7), and you will need to acknowledge the author and the title of the work in your article or book.

It's also worth making a note of sources you decide *not* to use (and why); you can easily forget over a period of time if you decided not to use a source, and then waste time locating it again only to find that it's not useful.

## DOING THE GROUNDWORK

Before you visit the local history section of the library or the local record office, it is worth doing some groundwork before you go. Most country libraries and record offices have websites (see Appendix 5 on page 199) which contain answers to most of the questions you might ask. These include:

- How to get there (if you can use public transport; parking availability and whether parking spaces need to be booked in advance)
- Whether you need a reader card. Many of the record offices operate the CARN system – standing for County Archive Reader Network; your CARN ticket can be used in any of those offices. It shows your name, address, signature, card number and expiry date (and it is valid for four years) and what documentation you need to bring to register for a card (usually something confirming your identity and address, e.g. a driving licence, recent utility bill or bank statement; as well as something with a signature, such as a bank card. Some offices may ask for a photograph.)
- Opening hours (including weeks when they are closed for stocktaking)
- Special needs' requirements (wheelchairs, loop systems for hearing aid users, large screens for people who have difficulty with sight)
- What documents they have (most have an online guide so you can check on the internet, though bear in mind this is only as good as the keywords in the database and there may be other relevant documents that don't contain those keywords in the database) and what format they're in (i.e. some are on microfiche or microfilm). If you are looking for specific documents, it's worth asking beforehand because the staff can tell you if they're available or if there are additional documents you might find useful

- Whether you need to book a seat in advance, and how long the slot is
- Whether you need to book a map table in advance, and how long the slot is
- Whether you need to book a microfiche/microfilm reader in advance, and how long the slot is (some record offices allow you a two-hour slot, others a half-day)
- Whether you are able to use a laptop on mains plug (some record offices will require advance booking for a seat with a power outlet; others will ask you for an electrical testing certificate for your laptop)
- Whether there are any restrictions on the material. For example, some documents at the National Archives are housed at a different site and you need to order them in advance; if the material is in a special collection, you may need permission from the owner of that collection to view it and use it
- Whether you can use a digital camera or tape recorder (if you plan to use one)
- If there are any information leaflets about the subject you want to research; they can save you time in locating references, and some leaflets may be available online
- Document production
    - What time the documents are available
    - How frequently they are fetched and when (some offices fetch documents on request; others fetch them at intervals, for example every half hour at quarter to and quarter past), and how long you can expect to wait before the document is produced (e.g. 20 minutes)
    - How many documents you can request at any one time, and whether you can request any in advance (this will save you time; even if you can't order documents in advance, an online index to their holdings may be available (see above) so you can at least have the references ready before you get there).

## VISITING THE RECORD OFFICE

Record offices usually ask you to sign a signing-in book on each visit. This is to acknowledge you have read the rules (which are there to protect the documents) and will abide by them. If you have a CARN ticket you will need to sign in with your name and ticket number.

There are some rules that all search rooms have in common. These are to protect the documents and also make sure that you take account of other users' needs. They include:

- No smoking
- No eating or drinking, including sweets or gum (debris and liquids can damage documents)
- Use pencils only (this is because ink, ballpoints and gel pens are not erasable and can damage documents; it's also best to avoid using pencil sharpeners and erasers because the debris can damage documents)
- Leave all bags, coats, umbrellas, folders, laptop cases, plastic bags and briefcases in lockers (the lockers often have coin-operated locks; check beforehand what you'll need so you have the right change to use the lockers)
- Switch off all mobile phones or put them on silent operation (and don't use them in the area)
- Silence in the room (so you don't disturb other researchers).

Things you will be allowed to take into the search rooms include:

- Laptop computers (but not the case)
- Notebooks and loose papers
- Pencils
- Glasses
- Money (e.g. for photocopying fees).

Some record offices give you a transparent plastic bag to hold your personal items while you're in the search room.

Once you've signed in and sorted out a reader card, if you're not sure where to get started one of the record office staff will show you how to use the index and catalogues, as well as where microfiches and films are kept and how to order documents.

Records that are used a lot (such as census returns), scattered through-out a wide geographic area (such as parish registers) or which are very fragile (such as back copies of newspapers) tend to be available in microfilm or microfiche format. Record office staff can show you how to use a microfilm reader and microfiche reader; until you get used to it, it can be tricky to load a film (particularly if a previous researcher didn't rewind it properly – in that case the entire film may be back to front), so do ask if you get stuck. The staff won't laugh at you or think you are a nuisance.

## What kind of documents do record offices hold?

Record offices often have an online catalogue, either accessible on their own website (see Appendix 5, page 199) or through Access to Archives (A2A – see www.a2a.org.uk). The kind of records you can expect to find include:

- Parish registers – births, marriages, deaths
- Census returns and census enumerator books
- Wills and probate records
- Churchyard surveys, cemetery registers and grave books
- Electoral registers
- Taxation and rating records – land tax, duty on land values, rate assessments, hearth tax assessments, window tax assessments
- Records of the poor – Guardians of Poor court books, poor rate books and assessments
- Title deeds and manorial records
- Maps – Ordnance Survey, tithe maps, enclosure maps, private estate maps, road order maps and deposited plans

- Sales particulars and catalogues
- Street directories and trade directories
- Building control plans
- Photographs, postcards and cartes de visite
- Ecclesiastical records – bishop's registers, visitation records, consistory court records, faculties, consecration records, glebe terriers, parish records (benefice papers, vestry minutes, churchwardens' accounts)
- Administration records – court rolls, assembly rolls and minute books, freemen's rolls and admissions books, apprenticeship registers and indentures, mayoral court books
- Legal records – quarter sessions minute books and files, coroners' inquests, registers of conviction, gaol chapel books, nominal registers, bridewell registers, charge books and minute books, calendars of prisoners (assizes, quarter sessions), cell books from town lockups, index of prisoners sentenced to transportation
- Hospital records – accounts, title deeds, admission registers
- Local newspapers
- Estate papers and personal papers (including letters, diaries, receipts)
- Antiquarian notes.

## WORKING WITH DOCUMENTS – PRACTICAL TIPS

Some of these are terribly obvious, but can easily be forgotten in the excitement of a search.

- Make sure your hands are clean and dry
- Handle the documents as little as possible (the grease from your hands can cause damage) and try not to touch written text
- Don't use a pencil to point out or follow entries, or put any other mark on the documents – use a piece of white acid-free paper instead under the line of text to help you keep your place (the record office will have these on request)
- Use pencils only for making notes. Avoid using a rubber or pencil sharpener among original documents – the debris can mark the documents

and make them illegible for other users, so use a propelling pencil or have a supply of ready-sharpened pencils before you go

◆ Put bound volumes on stands, wedges or cushions to support their spines, not flat on the table, and turn the pages carefully

◆ Make sure the whole document is on the table and nothing hangs over the edge (otherwise it's easy to damage documents)

◆ Don't rest anything (including your hand, notebooks, papers or magnifying glasses) on the documents – if your document is in a roll or outsize, the record office staff will give you special weights to use (they are either circular or sausage-shaped, with soft leather covers that won't mark or damage the documents)

◆ If you request a bundle of documents, make sure you return them in the same order as you found them and don't mix them up with other document bundles

◆ Take the documents back as soon as you've finished with them

◆ Make a note of the references you used before you start making notes – it will save you going over the same ground in a few months' time when you've forgotten that you looked at this particular document or bundle. If your search wasn't successful, make a note of what you looked for and that you failed to find it

◆ Return documents promptly

◆ When you have finished using the microfilm, wind it back onto the spool it was on originally and return it to the correct storage slot. You should also have a 'marker' (usually a coloured plastic box) to put in place of the box for that spool. The marker box has a label to show which film reading machine is using that film (e.g. if someone else wants to use it after you). It also helps you find the correct place more easily when you return the spool

◆ When you have finished using the microfiche put it back in the correct storage slot. When you take a fiche out, you should mark the place with one of the special markers stored next to your machine (as above, it will help other researchers know that that fiche is being used by someone else and will also help you return the fiche to the correct place)

◆ Check with record office staff if you wish to trace something. If possible, place a clear plastic sheet between the tracing paper and the document to save wear and tear on the document.

## Making copies

There are some restrictions on copying documents in a record office. Some documents can't be copied because:

◆ Copying will break the law of copyright (particularly with maps and illustrations)
◆ Copying could damage the binding of a book
◆ The document is too fragile or delicate to be copied.

It is often possible to have printouts from microfilm or microfiche (for a fee), and you may be able to arrange photographic copies of more delicate material (again, for a fee). Flash photography isn't usually allowed, and neither is the use of hand-held scanners.

## Avoiding the pitfalls

*Dating*

A year isn't always a year! Until 1752, the English calendar followed Church convention and the first day of the year was Lady Day (25 March). So to convert dates between 1 January and 24 March to modern dates, add a year onto the year given in a parish register. For example, 1 February 1710 in a parish register would be 1 February 1711 in a modern calendar. Historians note this date as 1 February 1710/11.

In 1752, the country switched from the 'old style' Julian calendar to the 'new style' Gregorian calendar. The Julian calendar (adopted by Julius Caesar) included every fourth year as a leap year. In 1582 Pope Gregory reformed the calendar so that it followed the solar year (with every fourth year except a centennial being a leap year) and cut 10 days from the calendar to adjust it. This calendar was known as the Gregorian calendar and was adopted by the Catholic countries in Europe. As England was a Protestant country, it kept to the Julian calendar rather than using the Gregorian calendar so, by 1752, dates in England were 11 days in front of the rest of Europe (and Scotland). Under the Calendar Act of 1752, England switched to the Gregorian calendar but had to lose the extra 11 days – so Wednesday 2 September 1752 was followed by Thursday 14 September 1752. The authorities were worried about losing 11 days' taxation, so those 11 'lost' days were added to the end of the financial year – hence the taxation year ends on 5 April (11 days after Lady Day). The financial year was moved back to 31 April in 1854 but the taxation year continues to run from 6 April to 5 April.

Some dates also refer to dates around Easter, such as the 10th day after Easter. As Easter is a moveable feast, you'll need to check the actual date in a list of tables (such as those by Cheney – see the list of useful books in Appendix 3 on page 175).

In some records, the year is recorded by regnal year. So something dated 3 George II would occur in the third regnal year of George II, i.e. in the period 1 August 1716 to 31 July 1717. (See Appendix 4, page 177 for a list of regnal years.)

In Quaker records, the months are recorded by number rather than name: either '3rd mo.' or 'III', for example . This can cause some confusion – before 1752 the first month was March, and after 1752 the first month was January, so follow the convention of using double years as above. Also note that the American usage of putting the month before the day (in numerical terms) is sometimes followed by Quakers.

*Numbers*
Before about 1640, most parish registers were written using Roman numerals or Latin words for dates. Where numbers are concerned, it's worth remembering that the last 'i' in a register may be shown as a 'j'.

| Number | Latin figure | Latin number | Latin date | English date |
|---|---|---|---|---|
| 1 | i or j | unus | primo | 1st |
| 2 | ii or ij | duo | secondo | 2nd |
| 3 | iii or iij | tres | tertio | 3rd |
| 4 | iv or iiij | quattuor | quarto | 4th |
| 5 | v | quinque | quinto | 5th |
| 6 | vi or vj | sex | sexto | 6th |
| 7 | vii or vij | septem | septimo | 7th |
| 8 | viii or viij | octo | octavo | 8th |
| 9 | ix or viiii or viiij | novem | nono | 9th |
| 10 | x | decem | decimo | 10th |
| 11 | xi or xj | undecim | undecimo | 11th |
| 12 | xii or xij | duodecim | duodecimo | 12th |
| 13 | xiii or xiij | tredecim | decimo tertio | 13th |
| 14 | xiv | quattuordecim | decimo quarto | 14th |
| 15 | xv | quindecim | decimo quinto | 15th |
| 16 | xvi or xvj | sedecim | deicmo sexto | 16th |
| 17 | xvii or xvij | septendecim | deicmo septimo | 17th |
| 18 | xviii or xviij | octodecim or dudeviginti | deicmo octo or duodevicesimo | 18th |
| 19 | xix | undeviginti | deicmo nono or undevicesimo | 19th |
| 20 | xx | viginti | vicesimo | 20th |
| 21 | xxi or xxj | | vicesimo primo | 21st |
| 30 | xxx | triginta | tricesimo | 30th |
| 40 | xl | quadriginta | | |
| 50 | l or L | | | |
| 60 | lx | | | |
| 70 | lxx | | | |
| 80 | lxxx | | | |
| 90 | xc | | | |
| 100 | c or C | centum | | |
| 200 | cc | | | |
| 500 | d or D | | | |
| 1 | m or M | | | |

So 1635 in Latin numbers is MDCXXXV.

Also note that if a date was written 7ber, it meant the 7th month –
which before 1752 was September.

*Latin days, months and time*
Days of the week in Latin:

| | |
|---|---|
| Monday | *dies lune* |
| Tuesday | *dies martis* |
| Wednesday | *dies mercurii or dies wodenis* |
| Thursday | *dies jove or dies iovis* |
| Friday | *dies veneris* |
| Saturday | *dies saturno or dies sabbatina* |
| Sunday | *dies sole or dies domini* |

Months of the year:

| | | | |
|---|---|---|---|
| January | *Januarius* | July | *Quintillis* |
| February | *Februarius* | August | *Sextilis* |
| March | *Martius* | September | *September* |
| April | *Aprilis* | October | *October* |
| May | *Maius* | November | *November* |
| June | *Junius* | December | *December* |

Latin phrases for time:

| | |
|---|---|
| *Anno domini* | In the year of the Lord |
| *Ante meridiem* | Before noon (a.m.) |
| *Altera die* | On the next day |
| *Cras* | Tomorrow |
| *Die sequenti* | On the next day |
| *Die vero* | On this very day |
| *Ejusdem die* | Of the same day |

| | |
|---|---|
| *Eodem anno* | In the same year |
| *Eodem die* | On the same day |
| *Eodem mense* | On the same month |
| *Hodie* | Today |
| *Mane* | In the morning |
| *Nocte* | At night |
| *Post Meridiem* | After noon (p.m.) |
| *Postridie* | On the day after |

*Handwriting*

The older a document is, the harder it can be to read. This is partly due to changes in letter formation, but also because earlier ages tend to use abbreviations that might not be familiar to the modern reader. Record office staff may be able to help you decipher the odd word, but won't have time to work with you on an entire document. If you are using a wide timespan, it's best to start with the later documents and work backwards – you will find it easier to see how the letters and abbreviations change.

It is also worth making yourself an 'alphabet' – look at words you know (such as names or some of the commonly used Latin words), pick out the letter formation of those letters, and list them alphabetically. This will help you work out unfamiliar words.

When transcribing from an original document, only write what's there – don't modernise the spelling. (Spelling wasn't standardised until the 18th century; you may also find names transcribed wrongly, misheard and even spelled according to dialect.) If you write out an abbreviated word in full, put square brackets round the letters you've added so you have a clear record of what's there. There are common abbreviations – C. T. Martin's *The Record Interpreter* is a superbly helpful resource here, as it gives Latin and French abbreviations, explains the conventions of abbreviations, gives a glossary of Latin words, and gives Latin versions of place names, first names and surnames.

*Money*

Figures can seem a bit meaningless because of inflation – see www.measuringworth.com/calculators.ppoweruk for a good way of showing how much something was worth in today's money. Be aware that it does depend on what you're looking at, and the value of property doesn't change in the same way as those of wages or bread. Lionel Munby, *How Much Is That Worth?*, is a good starting place for working out values.

*Money before 1971*

Guinea = 21 shillings

£1 (l) = 20 shillings (s) or 240 pence (d)

1 crown = 5 shillings

$\frac{1}{2}$ crown = 2 shillings and 6d (sometimes written as 2/6)

1 florin = 2 shillings

1 shilling = 12 pence

1 pence = 2 halfpennies (sometimes abbreviated to 'ob', from the Latin *obulus*)

1 pence = 4 farthings (sometimes abbreviated to 'qua', from the Latin *quadrans*).

In medieval times, you may come across other monetary references:

1 groat = 4 pennies (until 1662)

1 mark = 13 shillings and 4 pence or 2/3 of £1 (NB there was no actual coin called a 'mark' – it was a paper reference only)

1 noble = 80 pence or 6s and 8d (the angel, also worth 80d, superseded it in 1464).

Some of the coins also had nicknames:

◆ A halfpenny was known as a 'ha'penny'
◆ A two-pence piece was known as 'tuppence'

- A three-pence piece was known as a 'thruppenny bit'
- A sixpence was known as a 'tanner'
- A shilling was known as a 'bob'
- A ten-shilling piece was called a 'half-sovereign'
- £1 was known as a 'quid'.

*Money after 1971*

Britain switched to decimal coinage on 15 February 1971. For a while, some 'old money' coins were still legal tender, and the decimal penny was known as 'new pence' until about 1980 to distinguish it from old money.

- 6d was equivalent to $2\frac{1}{2}$p (the sixpence was abolished in 1980)
- a shilling was equivalent to 5p (the shilling was abolished in 1990)
- a florin was equivalent to 10p (the florin was abolished in 1992).

**Interpreting documents**

- Keep it in the context of contemporary events – for example, you may think a parish has a significant number of deaths. If that happens to be a plague year (or a period of another epidemic, such as cholera or smallpox) in the area, that will explain the increased death rate. Or if you are looking at a map, look at it from the point of view of people at the time the map was drawn – what we might think of as a steep, impassable route might still have been a route (albeit a difficult one) years ago
- Keep it in the context of the document. It is easy to extract small quotations to back up an argument, but if those quotations are taken out of context they might not mean what the original author intended, so look at the whole of the document if possible
- Ask yourself who created the document and why – for example, tithe maps were created by Tithe Commissioners and the purpose was to show cultivated land (on which a tithe was payable) and non-titheable

land (such as roads and highways), so more detail will be shown on the titheable land and some of the information on the non-titheable land may be missing because it was not relevant to the purpose of the Tithe Commissioners

◆ Ask yourself when it was created. For example, a map created in 1910 might not be an accurate representation of the same area in 1840 or even 1940, let alone today. Or a sketch of a house in 1850 might look very different from the same house 50 years later after the house had been extended or the frontage changed

◆ Ask yourself how it was created – what had to be done? For example, in compiling census information the enumerator had to visit every property in the district and note down the information required by law. Did that leave room for error? Yes, because the literacy of the householders varied – some didn't know how to spell names (and neither did some of the enumerators), some weren't aware of the ages or places of birth of visitors, and some people deliberately lied about the ages of their children because, for example, a 15-year-old would earn more money than a 12-year-old. Socially, too, there may have been reasons for not telling the truth: an illegitimate child may have been claimed as the grandparents' youngest child rather than as a grandchild. Could errors be put right? What was the process of correcting errors?

◆ Ask yourself who used the document and why. For example, window tax assessments were used by government officials to collect taxes. Indentures were used by masters to set out the terms of an apprenticeship – but were also used by the government for taxation purposes. Did anyone have any vested interest in not telling the truth and if so, why? (For example, if you didn't register the birth of a child within 42 days in England and Wales, a fine was payable – so it's likely that some records are not accurate in order to avoid the fine.) Were there any consequences if the records were found to be falsified and if so, what?

# 3

# Finding a Person

This chapter covers the kind of evidence that you could use to help you find out more about a person – what information each sort of evidence contains and where to find it, as well as highlighting potential difficulties with the evidence.

To begin with, think about why you want information about that person and how much detail you need – this will affect the sources you use.

- Biographical reasons (e.g. you're studying notable people in a region, such as town officials or owners of large businesses or clergy, or a nationally recognised figure such as Horatio Nelson) – start with secondary sources to pin down dates of important life events which you can then look up in primary sources.
- Leads regarding the history of a building or institution – secondary sources may be useful if this person is locally noteworthy; otherwise you will need to use primary records. For example, if I were studying the building in Norwich known as 'Bacon's house' at 31 Colegate, I know it once belonged to a former city mayor called Henry Bacon and would be able to find some information about Henry Bacon in secondary sources; but if I were looking at previous occupants of say my parents' house, I'd need to work back through primary sources such as title deeds and rate books to find out who the owners and occupiers were before I could look them up in secondary sources.

## LOOKING AT SECONDARY SOURCES

Secondary sources (such as biographies and biographical dictionaries) can give you basic dates and details of a person's life:

- Date and place of birth (or baptism if the birth wasn't registered)
- Name and occupation of parents
- Early career details (including dates: for example, the date of election to a political office or the date when someone became a peer)
- Date and place of marriage and spouse's name
- Names and dates of birth of children
- Date, place and cause of death.

These details can be a good framework to help you do more in-depth research in primary sources or in local/national newspapers. Secondary sources are usually available in your local library's reference section; as well as in printed form, some may be available in CD-ROM, and others may be available online. Online sources may be on subscription only, but some county library services have a special subscription for some sources so their members can log in from home using their library card number. Some county libraries also give free access to genealogical websites such as Ancestry.

Your local university may also have a local studies section within the faculty of history which has digitised versions or transcriptions of original documents; for example the University of East Anglia has 'Virtual Norfolk' at http://www.webarchive.org.uk/pan/12032/20051206/virtual norfolk.uea.ac.uk/, which includes documentary sources, interpretations and a glossary with bibliographical notes.

### Oxford Dictionary of National Biography (ODNB)

This contains 50,000 detailed biographies of people who shaped the country's history, including writers, artists, officers, clergy and some professionals. For example, Nelson's biography is very detailed, giving his date and place of birth, his parents' names and occupations, his nickname, where he was educated, a very detailed account of his career, his social life (including his relationship with Lady Hamilton), and an analysis of the man himself. There's also a list of published sources (letters, private papers and diaries), archived sources and pictorial sources – all of which could be followed up by someone who wanted to write a lengthy biography.

The ODNB is online at www.oxforddnb.com; check with your library to see if you're able to access it from home using the library's subscription.

### Who's Who (and Who Was Who)

*Who's Who* has been published annually since 1849. Originally it was a list of ranks and appointments and the names of the people concerned – including the Royal Household, members of the House of Peers and House of Commons, judges, archbishops, and British envoys abroad – although there were no biographical details. Current editions give details of where and when the person was born, marital status, children, where the person was educated, a brief résumé of career, any honours and awards. There's also a section for 'recreation'; for example, George Bernard Shaw listed his recreations as 'cycling and showing off'.

The companion to this is the 10-volume series of *Who Was Who*, which contains over 100,000 biographies of people who are no longer alive.

There may also be similar volumes for specific counties, for example *Who's Who in Norfolk* (Ebenezer Baylis, 1935) covers leading citizens in the 1930s and before.

### Kelly's Handbook

*Kelly's Handbook* was published annually during the 19th and 20th centuries as an alphabetical listing of the titled, landed and official classes. Each name in the book has a brief summary of their genealogy and career. Earlier editions may be available on CD-ROM from an archive book publisher. Note that this is not the same as *Kelly's Directory*, which is a listing of tradespeople and the main occupier of a property.

### *Whitaker's Almanack*

*Whitaker's Almanack* has been published annually since 1868 and gives monthly news summaries, obituaries of key figures, results of major sporting events, meteorological observations and key dates (religious, civil and legal). Some of the obituaries are more detailed than others, but all will give birth and death dates and the person's occupation.

## Local newspapers

Local newspapers may have information about the person you're searching for. The precise information obviously differs depending on the events concerned and the person's 'newsworthiness', but you may find:

- Information about events (for example, if someone was involved in a rescue, fire, or flood; or a bankruptcy, embezzlement or criminal trial)
- Advertisements (for businesses and/or property sales)
- Obituaries.

See Chapter 9 for more information about newspapers.

## Street directories

You may also be able to glean information from street directories – your subject may be mentioned in the 'potted history' section at the start of each town or village's directory listing, or may be listed as a resident or trader in the directory listings.

## Written biographies

As with the ODNB, you may find a lot is already known about your subject. Biographies will contain facts that you can confirm with other sources; there may also be a list of sources of letters, diaries and private papers which you can access at whichever archive holds the documents.

## Putting it into practice

With *Norwich: Street by Street*, I was looking at each street within the old city walls, who lived there, important buildings and important events. So if we take Henry Bacon as an example: I know that his house on Colegate is number 31. Various local sources mentioned that he was sheriff in 1548, mayor in 1557 and 1566; Pevsner (see Chapter 4, page 86) mentioned Bacon's house on Colegate and added that Bacon died in 1567; and a secondary source mentioned that during his term of office he altered the city seal, replacing the representation of the Trinity with the city arms.

These sources all gave me leads to follow up, such as:

- City records (particularly the mayors' court books) to see what Bacon did as mayor, especially as I knew that he was active during Kett's Rebellion in 1549 and might therefore have had a leading role in the conflict
- The City seal – I could check the ones before Bacon's term of office and those afterwards to see if there were any differences between them
- Guild records – I knew Bacon was a worsted merchant and clothier: did he make any specific changes to guild customs? Did he enrol any new apprentices?
- Parish registers – I knew Bacon was buried in St George's church in Colegate in 1567, so I could visit the church to see if there were any monuments to him, and check the parish registers around the time of his death to see if there was any information there about him
- Will – the indexes told me the reference to his will is PCC 22 March 1567/8; so checking the will might tell me what he left and to whom
- His will would give me further leads to follow up – details of property, so I could see what he owned and trace that back to when he bought it; or I could trace the family references forward and back via parish registers.

However, with the remit of that particular book, I knew I wouldn't have enough room to give Bacon a full biographical entry. I didn't end up tracing his will and descendants – but if I ever need to do so in the future, I have the references I'll need to start tracing them in my working notes.

## LOOKING AT PRIMARY SOURCES

These are the records that can help you trace someone's life (or ownership/occupation of a building):

- Parish registers (baptisms, deaths, marriages)
- Quaker records
- Clandestine marriages
- Ships' log books
- International Genealogical Index
- Boyd's Marriage Index
- Wills and probate records
- Census records (census returns and enumerators' books)
- Local census returns
- Electoral registers
- Taxation and rating records
- Apprentice records
- Business records
- Criminal and court records
- Poor relief/workhouse records
- School records
- Public health records
- Hospital records
- Manorial records.

## USING PARISH REGISTERS (BAPTISMS, DEATHS, MARRIAGES)

Before the civil registration of births, marriages and deaths was centralised in England and Wales on 1 July 1837, records of baptisms, marriages and burials were made in the church or chapel where they took place. These records are known as parish registers and they record baptisms, marriages, burials and banns in the Church of England from 1538 onwards. However, not all registers have survived and those dating before 1598 are likely to be copies of earlier books.

From 1 July 1837, all births and deaths had to be reported to a local registrar, who reported them to the superintendent registrar in the district. The superintendent kept one copy and sent a separate copy every three months to the Registrar General. With weddings, the church took two registers; one was kept by the church and the other was sent (once filled) to the superintendent registrar in the district. Every three months, the church official also sent a copy of entries in the register for the last quarter to the Registrar General.

For marriages in church, banns were called for three Sundays before the wedding in the church where the bride and groom were to be married, and if one of them lived in another parish the banns would also be called in the church of that parish. If the couple married by licence, the couple could marry on the same day as the licence was issued, or the day after. Licences were more expensive than banns. A special licence meant that the marriage could take place anywhere, but was rare because only the Archbishop of Canterbury or his officials could grant it. The common licence named one or two parishes where the marriage could take place, and could be issued by archbishops, bishops, archdeacons, ministers or officials entitled to act on their behalf (known as 'surrogates'). Licences were often accompanied by bonds, which were sworn statements by a couple's friends or relatives that:

- There was no impediment to the marriage
- The couple would marry in a specified church
- The bond money (i.e. how much money they would forfeit if the licence was not complied with).

## What information they contain

*Baptism registers before 1813*

- Date of baptism
- Child's name
- Parents' names (though sometimes only the father's name is given).

Some registers will include the father's occupation, the child's date of birth and the mother's maiden name.

*Baptism Registers 1813 onwards*

Baptisms were entered into pre-printed standard registers. Columns were included for:

- Date of baptism
- Child's name
- Parents' names
- Parish of residence
- Father's trade or occupation
- The name of the officiating minister.

Sometimes the date of birth and mother's maiden name were included.

*Marriage registers before 1754*

- Date of marriage
- Names of the bride and groom.

Sometimes the groom's occupation is listed.

*Marriage Registers 1754-1837*

As with baptisms, marriages were entered into pre-printed standard registers. Between 1754 and 1837, all couples had to marry in an Anglican church for their marriage to be legally valid; only Quakers and Jews were exempt.

The information recorded included:

- Date of marriage
- Names of the bride and groom
- Parish of residence for both bride and groom
- Whether the marriage was by banns or licence
- Whether the groom was a bachelor or a widower
- Whether the bride was a spinster or a widow
- Signatures of bride and groom, the officiating minister and two witnesses (those unable to write would make a mark).

There may be additional information, such as the groom's occupation or the name of the bride's father.

*Banns Registers after 1754*

The registers of the banns were kept from 1754. Before 1823 you should find them in the back of the marriage registers; after 1823 they were kept in separate registers.

The information in the banns included:

- Names of the bride and groom
- The three dates when the banns were read out in church.

They may also have recorded the bride and groom's place of residences, and if one of the spouses lived in another parish the banns register would also note that parish.

*Marriage Registers after 1837*

Births, marriages and deaths were registered centrally from 1 July 1837. Church marriage registers took on the same format as civil marriage certificates. The information includes:

◆ Marriage date
◆ Names of the bride and groom
◆ Parish of residence for both bride and groom
◆ Occupation (usually the groom and sometimes the bride)
◆ Ages ('of full age' usually means 21 years or over)
◆ Whether the groom was a bachelor or a widower
◆ Whether the bride was a spinster or a widow
◆ Name and occupation of the father of both bride and groom
◆ Whether the marriage took place by banns or licence
◆ Signatures of bride and groom, the officiating minister and two witnesses (those unable to write would make a mark).

*Burial Registers before 1812*
◆ Date of burial
◆ Name of person buried (family relationships may be given e.g. wife of, widow of, son/daughter of – this tends to be mainly in the case of women and children).

Sometimes the age at death and occupation was included. It may also be recorded if the person was from the workhouse ('pauper').

*Burial Registers after 1812*

As with births and marriages, burials were entered into pre-printed standard registers. Columns were included for:

◆ Date of burial
◆ Deceased's name

- Parish of residence
- Age at death
- Officiating clergy.

Clergymen sometimes added a family relationship e.g. wife of, widow of, son/ daughter of; this tends to be mainly in the case of women and children. Occasionally, the cause of death is listed – sometimes as 'p' or 'pest' if it was the plague. Some clerics give more information than others, e.g. if someone had been murdered the cleric might have recorded some of the details and whether the murderer was caught and paid the penalty.

### Where to find them

- County Record Offices (see Appendix 5)
- Family Records Centre (part of the National Archives) at 1 Myddleton Street, London EC1R 1UW – for union indexes of births, marriages and deaths registered officially in England and Wales from 1 July 1837 up to about twelve months ago. They're known as 'union' indexes because registration districts took their name from the poor law union in which they were based. You can search the indexes online for a small fee at www.findmypast.com – note that you will need to register, give a password and download a special viewer so you can use the indexes
- Scottish General Register Office – for indexes of Scottish registers of births, marriages and deaths since 1 January 1855 and of births and marriages in the Church of Scotland from about 1553. There is also a computerised link to these records at the Family Records Centre, or you can search online at www.scotlandspeople.gov.uk and view indexes of birth registrations 1855–1903, marriages 1955–1928 and deaths 1855–1953, again for a small fee
- Family History Societies may also have copies of the indexes.

## Potential difficulties

Before the 19th century there were no rules about how entries should be set out in the registers or what details should be included, so they are not consistent between parishes or even between different clerics in the same parish. There are also likely to be gaps during the period of the Civil War, 1645-60.

*Varying layout*

Usually entries are chronological. However, the layout varies – early registers tend to mix baptisms, marriages and burials, whereas later ones have baptisms at the front, marriages in the middle and burials at the back. Because parchment and paper were expensive, the clergy used all the space in the registers – so sometimes when the last page had been filled they squeezed entries into little gaps found earlier on in the registers.

*Entries in Latin*

Some parish register entries are in Latin (particularly those before the 18th century). Some of the most common phrases used are:

- *baptisatus / baptisata est / erat / fuit* – was baptised
- *natus/nata* – was born
- *filia* – daughter
- *filius* – son
- *gemini* – twins
- *conjuncti fuerant* – were joined in marriage
- *copulati sunt/erant* – were married
- *nupti erant* – were married
- *nupsit* – married
- *licentiam* – by license
- *bannum* – by banns
- *uxorem duxit* – he took to wife (i.e. married)
- *sepultus / sepulta* – buried

- *mortus* – died
- *eodem die* – on the same day (as the previous entry)
- *ultimo die mensis* – on the last day of the month of
- *primo die mensis* – on the first day of the month of
- *parochia* – parish
- *in comitatu/in agro* – in the county of
- *ibidem* – in the same place
- *extraneus* – a stranger.

*Dates*

Dates may be shown in Roman numerals (see Chapter 2, page 24, for more information about Roman numerals and Latin dates). There is also the problem of the calendar change in 1752 (see Chapter 2, page 22, for details about the date change and the accepted convention of writing dates before 1752).

*Registration difficulties*

Deaths tend to be registered because after 1837 you could only bury someone if you gave the church a death certificate or coroner's certificate. However not all births between 1837 and 1874 were registered because you didn't have to inform the registrar of a birth, and many people thought that a baptism was a legal alternative to registration. The 1874 Births and Deaths Act meant that you could be fined if you registered a birth more than 42 days after the event, or didn't register it at all: so birth dates might not be accurate because if parents were late in registering a birth they'd tell the registrar a different date in order to avoid a fine!

There is also the fact that you only had to live in a parish for three weeks before the cleric could describe you as 'otp' or 'of this parish'.

*Civil war and Commonwealth*

There are a lot of gaps in registers during the English Civil War and Commonwealth periods, because some priests had to leave their parishes for political reasons. From 1653–60, the Parish Register was responsible for the registers rather than the church; this was a person elected by the ratepayers who had been approved by local magistrates. Births rather than baptisms were recorded, and deaths rather than burials. Also from 1653–60, only marriages conducted by the local Justice of the Peace were legal, and notices of 'publication of intention to marry' were posted in the market place for three weeks before the wedding rather than having banns called.

*Negative print*

If you are using a microfilm or microfiche copy of records, it will be a negative print copy (i.e. white text on a black background) and this can be hard to read for a long stretch of time.

## USING QUAKER RECORDS

Under the Marriage Act of 1753, marriage in England and Wales from 25 March 1754 (until 1837) was only valid if it was performed in an Anglican church after banns had been read, or by licence. The exception was if the couple were Jewish, married overseas or members of the Religious Society of Friends (Quakers). Quakers and Jews kept records of their own ceremonies.

### What information they contain

The minute books contain records of births, marriages, deaths and burials from the foundation of the Society up until 1837.

Death and burial registers mention the person's age and parents.

### Where to find them

◆ National Archives (series RG8)
◆ Digest registers – Friends Library in London (see appendix 2 for address); also online at www.quaker.org.uk.

### Potential difficulties

Records refer to days and months by number, so for anything before 1 Jan 1752, remember that the calendar year began on 25 March. This means the 12th month is February, not December.

## LOOKING AT CLANDESTINE MARRIAGES

Before the Marriage Act of 1753 (which came into effect 25 March 1754), you could get married legally without a church service. A marriage was classed as 'irregular' if:

◆ Neither the bride nor groom belonged to the parish where they married
◆ They had not formally published their intention to marry (banns) or bought a licence from the bishop
◆ If the ceremony took place in a period forbidden by the church (such as Lent).

Clandestine marriages tended to take place in secret, away from where the bride or groom lived, without banns and often without a licence either. Reasons why people married in this way were to save money or avoid publicity (e.g. apprentices who wanted to get married before their apprentice term had finished), to marry without parental consent if they were under the age of 21, or if the groom was in the army. One place where clandestine marriages often took place was the 'Rules' or 'Liberties' around the Fleet Prison in Farringdon Street, London. Marriages took place in taverns, coffee-houses, churches and work-shops. Registers were kept from 1690 but the marriages were outlawed in 1754.

## Where to find them
National Archives, series RG7.

## Potential difficulties
The registers are indexed but weren't kept meticulously. Problems include:

- Forgeries
- False names
- Mistakes copied from other registers
- Duplicate entries
- Altered dates.

# USING SHIPS' LOG BOOKS
From 1854 masters of British ships had to keep log books of births, marriages and deaths of passengers at sea; until 1874 they were sent to the Registrar General of Shipping and Seamen in Cardiff, and after then they were sent to the Registrars of England, Wales, Scotland or Ireland (depending where the passengers/seamen came from). Records of births and deaths of crew were kept separately from records of passengers until 1891, when the logs merged.

## What information they contain
Ships' log books contain information similar to parish records for births, deaths and marriages.

## Where to find them
- National Archives – series BT 158, 159 and 160 for passenger logs before 1890; series BT 153, 154 and 155 for crew before 1890, and BT 334 for births and deaths for both 1891–1964.

## USING THE INTERNATIONAL GENEALOGICAL INDEX

The Church of Jesus Christ of Latter-day Saints is working on an ongoing project to build an International Genealogical Index (IGI) by extracting birth, baptism and marriage entries from records worldwide. It is useful if you're trying to trace someone who moved around a lot or you are trying to work out which one of several indexed registrations is the one you're looking for.

### What information they contain

The first six columns are the ones you can use to locate parish records:

- Column 1: surname and first name
- Column 2: name of parents or spouse
- Column 3: gender (M = male; F = female; H = husband; W = wife)
- Column 4: event (A = adult christening; B = birth; C = christening; D = death or burial; F = birth or christening of first known child, in lieu of marriage date; M = marriage; N = census; S = miscellaneous; W = will or probate)
- Column 5: date of event
- Column 6: place (town or parish).

### Where to find them

- Family History Centres from the Church of Jesus Christ of Latter-day Saints allow the public to see the registers, though a small fee may be payable (See Appendix 2 for contact details.)
- The IGI is also available at the Family Record Centre in London for the whole country (on microfiche) and online at www.familysearch.org
- County record offices or local studies centres may have microfiches for your county, neighbouring counties or even the whole of England and Wales; the library of the Society of Genealogists also has copies. (See Appendix 2 for contact details.).

## Potential difficulties

There may be transcription errors. The IGI doesn't contain every single parish register entry before 1837, and not all records are complete.

# USING BOYD'S MARRIAGE INDEX

Boyd's Marriage Index lists marriage entries from English parish registers between 1538-1867.

## What information they contain

The index is searchable by the names of the bride and groom. It records:

- Spouses' names
- Name of the parish
- Year of marriage.

## Where to find it

- Society of Genealogists (on microfilm)
- Origins Network website www.originsnetwork.com (pay per view)
- County record offices or local studies centres may have microfiches for your county.

## Potential difficulties

Boyd used transcriptions rather than originals so there is double the possibility of errors. The index only covers 16 counties. There are also some peculiarities in that names starting Kn were indexed under N, names starting Ph were indexed under F and names starting Wr were indexed under R.

# USING WILLS AND PROBATE RECORDS

Wills are the documents by which people dispose of their property after their death. From the early 1500s to around 1750, an inventory (known as a probate inventory) of the deceased person's estate was filed with the will – it was needed to assess the charges of the probate court.

Until 12 January 1858, probate (proving of a will) was handled by the church courts; after that date they were transferred to a civil court. There is a printed calendar compiled for England and Wales annually listing all proved wills, i.e. those made legally valid. If someone did not leave a valid will, there may be an administration grant.

The Statute of Wills 1540 meant that males over the age of 14 and females over the age of 12 could make a will; after 1837 they had to be 21 to make a will. Wills didn't count if they were made by lunatics, prisoners, traitors, heretics or slaves. Married women couldn't own property until the Married Women's Property Act 1882, so they could only make a will if their husband consented.

### What information they contain

Wills tend to state that they are the last will and testament of [person's name] of [address] in the parish of [parish name]; it sometimes adds the person's occupation. Then there's often some religious wording, and the appointment of executors (named, sometimes with addresses, occupations and relationship to the deceased). The will then says how debts and funeral expenses should be paid, then states how the estate will be distributed. The spouse is listed first, then children, then others. There may be specific bequests; and information about how the property would be divided up if any of the heirs died first.

Administrations contain the name of the person appointed to administer the estate (usually a widow, child or brother, though sometimes a creditor), and the date will give you an approximate idea of the date of death.

The indexes to wills and administrations give the dates (and sometimes places) of death of the named people.

Calendars of wills list the deceased's name, date of death, where and when the will was proved (or administration was granted), the name of the executor (or administrator) and the value of the estate (usually the figure before payment of debts or funeral expenses; and it may be listed as 'effects under £50'). It may give the occupation of the deceased, executor or administrator, and in the second half of the 19th century it may also list the addresses of the executor or administrator and any relationship to the deceased.

Probate inventories list and value household furnishings and other goods that belonged to the deceased (except for land and buildings), often room by room. They would also list farm animals and equipment, items used for trade, the contents of shops, clothing, debts owed and debts due.

## Where to find them

The printed calendars of proved wills are on microfiches in county record offices; they are also available at the Family Records Centre and the Probate Search Room. Copies of proved wills before 1858 may be available in your local record office; for example, Norfolk record office holds wills and administrations proved from the 1370s to 1858 on microfilm. Inventories would be held with the wills, usually among the church court records in county record offices.

Copies of wills and administration granted by civil probate registries in England and Wales since 1858 are held in the Public Searchroom, Principal Registry of the Family Division, 1st Avenue House, 42–49 High Holborn, London WC1V 6NP. You can try contacting your local probate office to see copies of wills and administrations from 1858 to the present, and your local records office or local studies department may have microfilm copies of the indexes to wills and administrations in England and Wales from 1858.

If you are looking for a will or administration grant between 1796 and 1903, you can start with the yearly indexes in the Family Records

Centre (series IR 27), or with the registers which record death duty payments (series IR 26). The registers show when and where a will or administration grant was made. Scottish death duty registers from 1804 are in the National Archives of Scotland (reference IRS 5–14).

Some pre-1858 wills (particularly those of wealthy people) were proved by the Prerogative Court of Canterbury (PCC). These wills, together with administrations granted by this court, are held by The National Archives and can be seen on microfilm at the Family Records Centre (National Archives) in London. You can search indexes online from the 1300s to 1858 at www.nationalarchives.gov.uk/documentsonline/ although there is a small fee to view the digital images of the wills.

**Potential difficulties**

Fewer than one in ten people made wills or had them formally approved, and death duty registers only record estates that are liable to tax (i.e. were worth over a certain amount).

Probate grants or letters of administration were often dated several months after the date of death.

Until 1898 the value of the estate in the calendars is for personal effects only, not real estate.

## USING CENSUS RECORDS

Since 1801 a census of the country has been made every ten years (except 1941 during the second world war).

From 1801–31, the census was basically a headcount of the numbers of people (male and female), houses and families in a parish or township; it was carried out by the overseer of the poor. The General Register Office (GRO) was set up in 1837, so from 1841 onwards the GRO

carried out the census using a team of temporary workers called enumerators. The enumerators gave out a form a couple of days before the
census, and the form was completed on the night of the census, listing
the name of everyone who spent that night in the house. Every village,
town and county was split into enumeration districts, with about 200
households in each enumeration district.

The enumerator collected the forms and helped householders who
couldn't fill them in. Then the enumerator copied the form into a book,
explained any extra or missing people (for example, if a platoon of soldiers was temporarily posted elsewhere), and signed the book before
sending it to the local registrar. The registrar checked the book, signed it
and sent it to the superintendent; who in turn signed it and sent it to the
Registrar General in London.

Census details are kept private for 100 years as they contain personal
information, so the last census to be made available for public viewing
was that of 1901. The next to be made available will be that of 1911, in
January 2012.

The census dates were:

- 1801 – 10 March
- 1811 – 27 May
- 1821 – 28 May
- 1831 – 30 May
- 1841 – 6 June
- 1851 – 30 March
- 1861 – 7 April
- 1871 – 2 April
- 1881 – 3 April
- 1891 – 5 April
- 1901 – 31 March.

## What information they contain

*Census returns 1830–31*

Simply a count by overseers of the numbers of people (male and female), houses and families in each parish or township. For the most part, they do not include names; but some enumerators made lists of names (which are available at county record offices; some family history societies have also published transcriptions).

*Census returns 1841*

- Name (only gives the first forename)
- Address (may be approximate, e.g. just the hamlet name, but may give street name)
- Approximate age
- Occupation
- Whether the person was born in same county as he/she was living in on the night of the census (if not, this may be S for Scotland, I for Ireland, or F for Foreign Parts; or a NK for 'not known').

*Census returns 1851 onwards*

- Name
- Address (streets, roads, this may also give house numbers and names; in 1891 this also included the number of rooms occupied by a family if less than 5)
- Exact age at last birthday
- Marital status ('condition' – 'mar' for married, 'u' for unmarried and 'w' for widow or widower)
- Rank, profession or occupation (children are often noted as 'scholars'; in 1891 there are also columns for employer, employed or 'neither employer nor employed' – the latter means 'self-employed'; in 1901 it's 'employer, worker or own account' and there's also a column 'if working at home')

- Relationship to the head of the house (eg wife, son, daughter, sister, brother, visitor)
- Parish and county of birth
- Notes (i.e. if person is deaf-and-dumb, blind, 'imbecile or idiot', or lunatic – by 1891 the last two categories are lumped together).

*Census enumerator books*

The front pages of the enumerator books describe the boundary of the enumeration district. The number of people enumerated is a running number on the left-hand side of each page; the house number might appear in the second column next to the street name, or is otherwise unlisted.

## Where to find them

*Cenus returns*

The originals for the 1841–91 censuses for England, Wales, the Channel Islands and the Isle of Man are kept in the Family Records Centre in London. However, the ones for your county should also be available in your local record office and in some local studies centres on microfilm or microfiche. You can also search digital images and transcriptions of the 1901 census at www.1901censusonline.com; it's free to search the indexes although you'll pay a small fee to see the census pages and transcripts. You can also search the 1891 census at www.ancestry.co.uk. The Society of Genealogists also holds copies of the returns 1841–61 and 1891 on microfilm.

Census returns for Scotland are at the General Register Office for Scotland, though there is a computerised index to the 1881, 1891 and 1901 census at the Family Records Centre. You can also search the indexes online for a small fee at www.scotlandspeople.gov.uk/.

It's also possible to buy CD-roms which cover the census returns for one county in a particular year, from specialist geneaology suppliers; you can also buy microfiche copies of registration sub-districts from the National Archives.

*Census enumerator books*
The originals (and a microfilm set for the whole of England and Wales) are kept in the National Archives at the Family Records Centre; however, the ones for your county should also be available in your local record office on microfilm.

## Potential difficulties

For 1841, full addresses are not always given and family relationships are not included. Ages of anyone over fifteen were rounded down to the nearest five years (so if someone was 44 their age would be recorded as 40), and birthplaces only show if someone was born in that county, or if that person was born in Scotland, Ireland or 'Foreign Parts'.

The census only lists the people who stayed at the house on census night. Places of birth are not always correct – the enumerator might have misheard them or spelled them wrongly. And people within the family may not be at home on census night: for example, servants who lived in at their place of work, people in the army and navy, or people in institutions such as workhouses, hospitals, schools and prison.

For the 1841 survey, the microfilm is a negative copy; it's quite hard to read white handwriting on a black background.

It's also possible that ages are inaccurate; some women didn't want to admit that they had married a much younger man, and children are often shown as older than they really are because they could earn better wages as a 15-year-old, say, than as a 12-year-old. Family relationships could also be inaccurate; a woman's illegitimate child was often described as being the youngest child of her parents.

## USING LOCAL CENSUS RETURNS
Some cities also took a census of their poor. For example, in 1570 there was a census in Norwich. It was taken in order of parish.

*What information they contain*
- Name
- Age
- Comments (e.g. who he worked with, how he treated his wife)
- Spouse's name, age and occupation
- Children's names and occupations
- Where they live
- The verdict.

For example, in the parish of St Peter Southgate, there's an entry: 'Richard Rich of 35 yeris, a husbondman that worke with Mr Contrell, & kepe not with his wufe but at tymes & helpeth her little... They have dwelt here 2 yeris... The house of Mr. Robert Suklyng. *No almes & Veri poore. Hable to work. To go Away.*'

In sharp contrast, in the parish of St John Timberhill: 'Gefry Roberdes of 40 yeris, cordwainer in worke & diseased with the stone, & Anne, his wife, that botchetch; & 3 daughters, the eldes 9 yers and spyn & the rest to skole, & hath dwelt here ever.' He didn't get alms, but he wasn't asked to leave the parish.

### Where to find them
Local record offices; sometimes records are published by local record societies. For example, *The Norwich Census of the Poor*, published by the Norfolk Record Society in 1971.

### Potential difficulties
As with many records, survival may be patchy; there may be copyright, access and legibility issues.

## USING ELECTORAL REGISTERS
Electoral registers (sometimes called the Electoral Roll) record the names of people who are entitled to vote. They are arranged in order of electoral division, polling district and then alphabetically by voter or street. The series of registers starts in 1832, when they had to be deposited with the Clerk of the Peace.

### What information they contain
Names and addresses.

### Where to find them
Local studies libraries and county record offices have collections of registers. Some will be original; others will be on microfilm or micro-fiche. Other archive sources that have copies include the British Library; the National Archives; and the Society of Genealogists.

### Potential difficulties
Not all registers survive; because they were large, they were often thrown away when they were no longer current.

Earlier registers will be smaller because fewer people were entitled to vote. It's worth noting the dates of enfranchisement:

- From 1832 – in the boroughs, all male householders (i.e. including tenants) of land worth at least £10 a year, and in the counties owners of property worth at least £10
- From 1867 – in the boroughs, all owners of dwelling houses and occupiers who paid more than £10 in rent a year, and in the counties

all male householders of property worth £5 or who occupied land and paid rent of more than £50 a year

◆ From 1884 – all owners of dwelling houses and occupiers who paid more than £10 in rent a year (so this is most men over 21)

◆ From 1918 – all men over the age of 21; all women aged over 30 who were householders or wives of householders

◆ From 1928 – all women over the age of 21.

Note that not everyone registers to vote, so electoral registers will never be complete.

## USING TAXATION AND RATING RECORDS

Records of taxation – which identify taxpayers, people who were exempt from tax and people who were in arrears of payment – survive from medieval times. There were different types of taxes and the records were kept by different people.

The National Archives has a database of taxation lists in England between the late 1300s and 1689; this is online at www.nation alarchives.gov.uk/e179.

*Land Tax Assessments*

Land tax was levied each year between 1692 and 1949 (though the tax itself wasn't abolished until 1963); the Clerk of the Peace in each county kept the copies of the land tax assessments. The tax was based on 4 shillings in the pound and was levied on land with an annual value of more than £1 a year. Catholics had to pay double between 1692 and 1831. From 1798, landowners could sign a contract with the Land Tax Commissioners to pay a lump sum or buy government stock in exchange for freeing them from liability.

*Hearth Tax Assessments*

In 1662 there was a tax of two shillings for every fire, hearth or stove in households; it was payable in two instalments, at Michaelmas (29 September) and Lady Day (25 March). The tax was difficult to collect and was very unpopular; it was abolished after March 1689. There were exemptions:

- Houses rented at less than £1 a year
- Houses containing less than £10 of goods
- Hospitals
- Almshouses
- Paupers (if they had a certificate of exemption signed by the parish priest and churchwarden).

*Poll taxes*

Poll taxes were collected in 1377, 1379 and 1381, then again after restoration of the monarchy in 1660, 1667, 1678, 1689, 1691, 1694, and 1697. The charge was based on people's social rank, occupation or office. It varied between poll taxes:

- In 1377 it was 4d per person aged over 14
- In 1379 it was 4d per person over 16
- In 1381 it was a shilling per person over 15 (and this led to the Peasant's Revolt)
- For the 17th-century taxes, people over the age of 16 paid a shilling (if they weren't otherwise chargeable) and children under 16 paid 6d. Paupers were excluded.

*Window taxes*

The window tax was collected from 1696 to 1851. There was a flat rate house tax for part of these years, plus an amount which varied with the rateable value of the house. There was also a tax on the number of windows, which again varied:

- 1696–1766, on houses with 10 or more windows
- 1766–1825, on houses with 7 or more windows
- 1825–1851, on houses with 8 or more windows.

Windows of business premises were exempt in some years. The occupier rather than the owner had to pay the tax, but people who didn't have to pay poor rates were usually exempt. Many people blocked up windows so they didn't have to pay tax.

*Domesday books*
In 1910 (under the Finance Act) all properties in England and Wales were valued, and the registers were called the 'Domesday Books' (sometimes the 'Lloyd George Domesday Books'). For more details, see Chapter 7, page 127, Field Office Valuations.

*Poor Rate Assessments ('rate books')*
Before 1834 property-holders had to pay a rate to the parish to help keep the poor. (See below for more information about poor relief.) The overseers of the poor in each parish kept accounts of the rate paid in special rate books. During the 1800s, the rate was collected by the Boards of Guardians; in 1925 collection of the rates became the responsibility of the district councils. Poor rate assessments survive from the mid-1600s until the mid-1900s.

## What information they contain
*Land Tax Assessments*
- Names of landowners of property worth £1 (i.e. 20 shillings) a year or more
- Names of the owner/occupier of property
- Names of tenants.

The 1798 assessments show which landowners signed the contract to free them from liability and also list the contract number. Contracts made from 1905–1950 include plans of the property.

*Hearth Tax Assessments*

◆ Names of chargeable and non-chargeable households, arranged by county and then by parish
◆ The number of hearths in the house
◆ How much they had to pay.

Sometimes the returns (the actual amounts paid) were listed separately; in some lists the returns are marked on the assessments.

*Poll tax lists*

◆ Names of people who paid the tax
◆ How much they paid.

Some may also list occupations and relationships between household members.

*Window tax returns*

◆ Name and address of taxpayers
◆ Number of windows in the house
◆ Tax paid.

*Domesday books*

◆ A brief description of the property
◆ Name of the property owner and occupier
◆ The property's value.

Some are shown on large scale Ordnance Survey maps – see Chapter 7.

*Poor Rate Assessments*

Early lists show only the occupier's name and the sum assessed; even later books might not have a full description of the property – it might be simply listed as 'cottage'. From 1834, the names of owners and the rate assessments tend to be in separate books.

## Where to find them

*Land Tax Assessments*

County record offices, on microfilm or microfiche (usually in quarter sessions – in the records of the Clerk of the Peace); or for the 1798 assessments see the National Archives, series IR23 and IR24.

*Hearth Tax Assessments*

Assessments for Michaelmas 1662 to Lady Day 1666 and for Michaelmas 1669 to Lady Day 1674 are in the National Archives, series E179; other years are held in county record offices, either on microfilm or microfiche. Between 1666 and 1669 the tax was collected by commissions (freelance collectors, known as 'farmers') and few lists of taxpayers survive for that era.

*Poll Tax Lists*

Poll tax lists for the 14th century plus those for 1660, 1667 and 1678 are held in the National Archives in series E179; later ones are in series E182. County record offices hold some poll tax lists.

*Window tax returns*

Returns are generally in the county record offices.

*Domesday books*

Held in county record offices; also in the National Archives.

*Poor Rate Assessments*

These are held in county record offices.

## Potential difficulties

*Land Tax Assessments*

Not every householder's name is documented after 1798 because some paid the lump sum to avoid future taxation. Survival of records before 1780 is patchy.

*Hearth Tax Assessments*

The number of hearths might be inaccurate, and might change from one assessment to the next. Not every householder's name is documented because of widespread evasion.

*Poll Tax Lists*

Not everyone is documented, due to widespread evasion of the tax. The 14th-century lists are in Latin.

*Domesday books*

Survival of records can be patchy and county record offices may not have all maps available.

*Poor Rate Assessments*

Survival is patchy – it's unusual to find a complete set of rate books – and details aren't always accurate.

## USING APPRENTICE RECORDS

The 1583 Statute of Apprentices meant that people were forbidden to practise a trade or craft unless they had undergone a period of apprenticeship: that is, training. If you practised without having done an apprenticeship or being a member of a guild (see below), you could be fined.

### How apprenticeships were made

An apprenticeship usually started when someone was twelve or fourteen and lasted for seven or eight years; for pauper children, an apprenticeship might start at the age of seven (a minimum of age nine from 1847) and finish at the age of 21 (24 for boys before 1768). An indenture was signed – this was the record of the contract. Two copies of the indenture were signed: one by the child's parent or guardian, and one by the master. For pauper apprentices, two copies were signed by the parish overseers and the master of the apprentice, and they were signed by the Justice of the Peace. One copy went to the master and the other to the parish. The master agreed to give the child food, clothes and housing, do the child's laundry, and teach him or her a trade; in return the child's parent/guardian (or parish) would give the master a sum of money (the premium).

## Taxation on apprenticeships

From 1710 to 1804, a master who took on an apprentice had to pay stamp duty on the premium, which included housing, food and clothes as well as the training. The duty was 6d in the £ for premiums under £50, and 1s in the £ for premiums over £50. It had to be paid within a year after the end of the apprenticeship, either in London (where it was recorded in the City Registers) or to a local agent (where it was recorded in Country Registers). There were exceptions to the stamp duty:

- 'Poor law' apprentices (pauper children who were sent out by their parish to learn a trade)
- Apprenticeships set up by public charities.

## What information they contain

The stamp duty records are in the registers of the Commissioners of Stamps in London. They include:

- The date and amount paid
- The name, address and occupation of the master
- The name of the apprentice (and before 1752 the name of the apprentice's father or guardian, parish of residence and occupation)
- The date the indentures were signed
- The date the apprenticeship started and how long it lasted for
- Details of any changes to the terms (such as transfers or assignments)
- The premium paid for the apprenticeship (or sometimes, if no money had been paid, an estimate of its value).

Indentures for pauper apprentices usually contain details of:

- Name of the overseers
- Name of the master
- Name of the churchwardens
- Name of the justice
- Name of the apprentice
- The length of the apprenticeship
- The consideration (how much was paid to the master)
- Any conditions (e.g. that the apprentice could not marry without the master's permission, and would be given clothes for Sundays and holidays as well as for working days).

Indentures for apprentices usually contain details of:

- Name of the master (and his trade)
- Name of the apprentice (and sometimes date and place of birth)
- Name of the apprentice's father (and sometimes the address and occupation)
- The length of the apprenticeship
- The consideration (how much was paid to the master)
- Any conditions.

Records of people who were fined for trading without a prior apprenticeship are in the quarter sessions records at county record offices.

### Where to find them

Stamp duty registers (known as the *Apprenticeship Books*) – National Archives, series IR1. There are indexes to these at the National Archives and the Society of Genealogists.

There is no central register for indentures, although some local registers have been published. The indentures themselves (those that survive) are in local record offices, and copies are often on microfiche or microfilm. If a charity helped to pay the apprentice's premium, there may be mention in the charity's records in local record offices.

## Potential difficulties

For the stamp duty registers: as with many taxes, evasion was a problem, so not all the apprenticeships are listed. Note that indentures are often dated in regnal years; and, as with parish records, microform copies are negative – reading white text on a black background can be very tiring. The indentures themselves are often partly pre-printed but there may be legibility issues with the handwriting.

# USING BUSINESS RECORDS

As well as records of apprenticeship, you may find a lot of information in business records – either in the company records of the business itself, or in organisations such as:

* Craft guilds – these were voluntary associations of craftsmen and regulated each craft or trade. They covered apprentices (trainees), journeymen (who hired themselves out on a daily basis) and master craftsmen. The guilds controlled who was admitted (and therefore who practised the trade). Some set up schools; others made provisions for sickness, old age, widows and children. Many guilds ceased by the end of the 1700s or became charitable bodies.
* Livery companies – these were guilds in London; senior members wore a uniform (or livery). They normally had a master, wardens (elected every year), a court of 20 assistants, liverymen (who could become assistants), freemen and apprentices. They worked in the same way as guilds.

Some professions also had registers. Information about barristers will be in the admission registers of the Inns of Court in London. Bishops issued licences to medical practitioners, and apothecaries and GPs had to be registered from the 19th century.

Taverns and inns also had to be licensed; Justices of the Peace issued licenses through quarter sessions, often with a bond of surety (sometimes called recognizances) for the orderly keeping of the house, which were kept in registers. Licensing legislation changed between 1828 and 1869 so records and registers didn't have to be kept; a new licensing system was brought in from 1869 and registers of licenses were kept from 1872.

## What information they contain

- Livery companies – lists of officials, accounts, minutes of courts etc.
- Guilds – accounts, lists of guild members, minutes, For example, in the Guild of St George records 1389–1547 (published by the Norfolk Record Society, 1936), for 5 April 1547, there's a list of those present, a note of how much was paid and by whom for the guild feast, a lease of land to John Golde 'to bild & ediffie upon the same ground next Tumlond a sufficient house off xl ffoote longith ffor a dwelling house', and then the election of officers and admittance of almsmen
- Licences for medical practitioners – name, parish, date of issue and fee
- Registers of apothecaries – name, date of licence, place of residence
- GP registers – registration date, name, residence, qualification
- Tavern and inn recognizances – name of licensee, parish, name of person standing surety, alehouse name.

## Where to find them

- Business records: archives of the business concerned or in the county record office – you could also try the Business Archives Council, http://www.businessarchivescouncil.org.uk/contact/ .There may also be information about businesses in the local papers, for example when businesses first set up, bankruptcies and advertisements

- Guild records – county record office (some record societies have published local guild records)
- Livery companies – they hold their own records, so you'll need to apply to the clerk of the company. Some have also been published (see the Guildhall Library and Society of Genealogists library)
- Inns of court registers – Inns of court; also solicitors will be listed in the Law Lists (Brown's *General Law List* 1775–1801, and *The New Law List* and *The Law List* after then)
- Licences for medical practitioners – bishops' registers in county record offices (there are also some at the Wellcome Library for the History and Understanding of Medicine)
- Registers of apothecaries and GPs – Society of Apothecaries' register and GP registers on microfiches in the library of the Society of Geneaologists
- Tavern and inn recognizances – quarter sessions records in county record offices; also some family history societies publish licensing records.

## Potential difficulties

Company records vary – some are very extensive, and some are very limited in details. Many company records aren't indexed so you may have to search through a lot of records to find what you're looking for.

# USING CRIMINAL AND COURT RECORDS

Major crimes and some civil cases were tried at the assizes, which were generally twice a year (February to March and July to August). The records for these are held centrally at the National Archives. The kind of crimes tried at the assizes include:

- Murder
- Manslaughter
- Arson
- Theft

- Riot
- Rape
- Rebellion
- Treason
- Manufacturing counterfeit coins
- Burglary.

However, it's worth noting that the types of cases dealt with at the assizes depend on the position of the law, which changes over the years. For example, sheep-stealing would have been dealt with at the assize courts before 1830; when it stopped being a capital offence (i.e. punishable by death), it was dealt with by the courts at the quarter sessions or petty sessions. Middlesex didn't have an assize circuit and the cases were dealt with at the Old Bailey (which also dealt with London cases).

Lesser crimes were tried by the justices of the peace at a court known as the quarter sessions, which were held four times a year. Quarter sessions were also where county government business (such as the building and maintenance of roads, bridges, hospitals and civil business) was conducted, until county councils were created in 1889.

Petty sessions are equivalent to magistrates' courts.

Prison records (including records for Bridewells and lockups) may also be available, ranging from minute books to gaol chapel books, keeper's daily journals, surgeon's journals, diet record books, committee records, and nominal registers. In some counties, each gaol and Bridewell was assigned to a committee of visiting justices who had to inspect the prison and report back to the quarter sessions on conditions in the prison.

Other records include coroners' inquests, police charge books and police crime registers.

After a trial finished and a sentence was given, friends and relatives could petition for clemency. If clemency was given, it could reduce how severe the sentence was, i.e. commute (change) a death sentence to transportation, or reduce the number of years the prisoner was to be transported, or commute a sentence of transportation to a prison sentence, or reduce the number of years the prisoner was meant to be imprisoned.

## What information they contain

*Assize records*

Indictments – the name of the accused, description, address, offence (and date), and the name of the victim. The plea, verdict and sentence are sometimes added later.

*Quarter session records*

Quarter sessions records include:

- ◆ For crimes – information about the crime, petitions to the magistrates and records of examinations (witnesses, accused and victim), records of conviction
- ◆ For civil business – information roads, bridges and transport; lunatic asylums and hospitals; the poor and workhouses; prisons (including reports from the committee of visiting justices); the local militia; other civil business such as apprentice records, taking oaths and licensing of trades
- ◆ For debtors – writs of *distringas* (issued to a bank or company to stop the transfer of stock or payment of dividend), schedules of individuals' property, discharges.

There is a lot of information about daily life and historical detail in the quarter sessions records, and they sometimes include lists of prisoners from the assizes as well as quarter sessions. Some books include the sentences of people appearing at the sessions.

Petitions tend to have a list of names attached, as well as personal letters. They contain all kinds of information, for example, information about the prisoner's background, the prisoner's occupation or social status, and background to local crimes such as poaching, attacks on workhouses and factory machinery.

*Petty session records*

Petty session records include registers of convictions.

*Prison records*

Surgeon reports include names of prisoners who died in prison. Nominal registers vary in details but may include:

- Prisoners' names
- Date and place of committal
- Date and place of trial and of conviction
- Offence
- Sentence (e.g. transportation)
- Education
- Age
- Height
- Colour of hair
- Trade or occupation
- Religion and birth place
- Number of previous convictions
- Date of discharge
- Photographs (for late 19th-century registers onwards).

*Other records*

Police crime registers (registers of indictable offences) include:

- Date crime was reported
- Classification of offence

- Where and when the offence was committed
- Details of the person against whom the offence was committed
- Details of the accused
- Result.

## Where to find them

*Assize records*

National Archives (mainly in series Just 3 for records before 1559 and ASSI 1–54 for English records after 1559, ASSI 57–77 for Wales since 1559), or the National Library in Wales; calendars of prisoners from the assizes may be available at county record offices on microfilm or microfiche. Much of the Old Bailey material is online at www.old baileyonline.org.

There are also important secondary sources:

- The *Notable British Trials* series – for large trials (mainly murders), giving detailed information about the trial and witnesses' evidence
- The *Newgate Calendar* (1730–1850) – contains accounts of trials and lives. It may be available in your local studies library, and is also available online at www.exclassics.com
- British Trials 1660–1900 – these are on microfiche at the Guildhall Library and consist of pamphlets and reports about trials. They tend to be cases of murder, treason and highway robbery but also include defamation and divorce cases.

*Quarter session records*

These are often on microfilm at county record offices. Some counties have published their quarter sessions records; family history societies sometimes have indexes to the records.

*Petty session records*

These are held at county record offices.

*Prison records*

These are held at county record offices. The National Archives (HO 26 and HO27) has criminal registers for England and Wales, listing those charged with offences, date and places of trial, verdict and sentence if convicted, name of prison hulk (ship) for those transported. There may also be a physical description and the date of birth. The records are arranged in order of year, then by county within the year. The National Archives also has calendars of prisoners.

*Other records*

County record offices.

## Potential difficulties

*Assize records*

Records before 1732 were in Latin, heavily abbreviated and the handwriting is difficult to read; many are lost.

*Quarter session records*

Preservation of records tend to be patchy; those before the mid 1600s are less likely to be available, though many are in good preservation from the 1800s. Some courts authorised the destruction of previous records. For example, in Norfolk in 1879 the court ordered the destruction of the post-1800 sessions files.

*Petty session records*

Magistrate records less than 30 years old are not available to public view; records for the petty sessions don't tend to be well preserved.

*Prison records*

These records may be patchy. Also records up to 100 years old may be closed to the public.

*Police records*

Material available depends on the date the local police force was set up; they may not be catalogued or indexed.

## USING POOR RELIEF/WORKHOUSE RECORDS

Under the poor law legislation of 1598 and 1601, the parish vestry had to give 'relief' to the poor of the parish (e.g. tinkers, hawkers, evicted tenants, discharged soldiers, and people who were blind or lame). This could be through 'doles' of money, or paid in kind (such as fuel, food or clothes).

There were two kinds of relief:

◆ Outdoor – the paupers continued to live in their own home (or that of a relative) and were given money, food, clothing and goods. The able-bodied might also be given work; for example, men might repair roads and buildings, and women might do laundry and look after the sick
◆ Indoor – the sick, elderly and orphans were looked after in work-houses.

The Poor Law Act of 1601 said that relief could only be given to paupers in their parish of legal settlement – that is, a place where they had lived for at least a month. Because this meant people could move to richer parishes to claim poor relief, the Poor Law Relief Act of 1662 (sometimes known as the Settlement Act) introduced stricter rules, where someone was only entitled to relief if:

◆ They held public office or paid the parish rate
◆ They rented property in the parish worth over £10 a year
◆ They were unmarried but had worked in the parish for a year
◆ They were a woman who had married a man of the parish

◆ They were a legitimate child aged under 7 whose father lived in the parish

◆ They were an illegitimate child born in the parish

◆ They were apprenticed to a master in the parish

◆ They had lived in the parish for 40 days after giving the parish authorities prior written notice.

If someone was likely to be a burden to the parish and didn't meet the above criteria, they could be made to leave the parish and return to where they were legally settled. The Justice of the Peace would issue a pass recording their parish of legal settlement and they would be escorted by the parish constables through each parish between the one that had ejected them and their legal settlement.

There were often disputes between parishes over legal liability for a pauper, and the records of these are in the assizes papers. Because this act made it hard for people to move about in search of work, there was another Settlement Act in 1697 which let the overseers give a certificate of settlement to parishioners who wanted to move, saying that they would be accepted back in the parish if they needed poor relief.

In 1834, Earl Grey's government passed the Poor Law Amendment Act, which meant that the parishes of England and Wales were grouped together into 'poor law unions' (Scotland had different legislation). Instead of getting outdoor relief from the parish, the poor had to go into 'union' workhouses. The workhouses were built and run by the Board of Guardians of the Poor. Men, women and children were placed in separate blocks, so families were divided.

In 1930, the local authorities took over the poor law from the Boards of Guardians, which were abolished. The Poor Law Act was finally abolished in 1948, when many workhouses became hospitals.

## What information they contain

*Minutes/overseers' accounts/poor books*

- Money and goods given out
- The pauper's name
- What was given and when.

*Admission/discharge books*

- Name
- Age
- Occupation
- Marital status
- Parish of settlement
- Religion
- Date of admission/discharge
- Sometimes a description of the person
- The reason why relief was granted.

*Minutes of meetings*

These also include Guardians' correspondence.

*Punishment books*

- Name
- Date
- Punishment received
- Reason for punishment.

Some workhouses may also have had rules: for example, about diets, uniforms, the kind of labour the poor had to do, times for visiting other family members in the workhouse, and whether silence had to be kept at certain times during the day. Lists or pamphlets of these rules sometimes survive.

Workhouses also had to keep registers of births, baptisms, deaths and burials; every six months they had to list the names of paupers admitted, the date of birth and the amount of time they'd spent at workhouse.

### Where to find them

- County record offices – for union records 1834–1930, including admission and discharge registers.
- Local press – for information about the creation of workhouses.
- National Archives – Poor Law Commission records.
- Family history societies – some have indexed records.

### Potential difficulties

The details in the admission register might be untrue; the 'pauper' might have had to lie to be sure of getting poor relief (i.e. admission to the workhouse). Not all records survive.

## USING SCHOOL RECORDS

Before 1833 schools were voluntary; they were funded locally, through charitable grants of money and buildings. In the 19th century, the church and charities set up more schools, and there were also schools set up in workhouses. 'Ragged' schools were set up from around the 1820s to teach the children of the very poor (for free). From 1833, a £20,000 grant was made towards the education of poor children (through National and British schools). In 1870, the Education Act created school boards to step in where the voluntary schools were inadequate; however, the board schools charged fees and it also meant that the child wouldn't be out earning money, so the children of the poor didn't tend to go. By 1880, all children under 13 were supposed to go to school (though there were some exemptions); in 1891, the government released more funds so elementary school was free for all children. In 1902, the Education Act (Balfour's Act) put the control of elementary schools under the control of local authorities, who could also set up secondary education. The minimum age for leaving school was 14 in 1918, and 15 in 1947. From 1974 onwards, outside London, education became the responsibility of county councils and metropolitan councils.

## What information they contain

School board records include minutes and annual reports of the clerk to the board.

School headteachers kept log books, which were daily records of what happened in the school. They were usually confidential and were returned to the authorities when the school was closed. These contain details such as:

◆ The number of pupils
◆ Their attendance (and reasons for mass non-attendance such as epidemics or bad weather)
◆ Any problems with parents, children and staff
◆ General information about teachers
◆ Visits by local clergy, gentry or inspectors
◆ School events
◆ Any punishments (though these may be kept in separate books – these will list names, dates, what they did and what the punishment was)
◆ Details of the school buildings
◆ Financial arrangements and inspections.

School admission registers (from the mid-1800s) list information such as:

◆ The child's name
◆ The child's age
◆ The dates the child joined and left the school
◆ The names and address of the child's parents.

Information from the Education Act 1902 contains details about the inspection of schools, administration of endowments, and teacher training schemes.

## Where to find them

School records can be found at the National Archives – series ED2, ED3, ED4, ED16. ED18 and ED21.

Records for public schools are likely to exist in the archives of the school; records for charity schools and nonconformist schools are likely to be held in the county record office (or, for Quaker schools, in the library of the Society of Friends); records for workhouse schools will be with the other workhouse records (see the section on poor relief above). Records for parish schools don't tend to have survived before the 1800s, but the remainder will be found in county record offices.

Minutes and reports from school boards are kept in county record offices.

School admission records may be kept at the school or in county record offices if the school has closed; large schools (especially public schools) have published their registers, and copies of these are available at the library of the Society of Geneaologists.

You can also find lists of schools (and their headteachers) in street directories (see chapter 8); there may also be information in the Victoria County History, and you may be able to see the buildings on town plans or Ordnance Survey maps (see Chapter 7).

You may also find information in the local press when the school was first planned and opened.

## Potential difficulties
Not all records survive.

# USING PUBLIC HEALTH RECORDS
There were various epidemics in the early 19th century – particularly cholera and smallpox – and the Poor Law Commission made some investigations into public health. A more extensive survey was published as the Report on the Sanitary Condition of the Labouring Population 1842. The Royal Commission on the Health of Towns was appointed in 1843, and the Public Health Act was passed in 1848; after that, ratepayers could choose to establish a local board of health. The Ministry of Health was finally established in 1919.

The parish vestry paid for some medical treatment for the poor, and there are records of contracts with local doctors.

## What information they contain
- Information about setting up local boards of health – petitions to establish them and disputes about the petitions
- Local reports to the General Board of Health 1848–57 – information about outbreaks of disease, drainage and toilet facilities, water supplies, housing and overcrowding.

## Where to find them
- Information about setting up local boards of health – National Archives, series M13
- Local reports to the General Board of Health 1848–57 – microfiche in National Archives
- Contracts with local doctors to treat the poor – county record offices (may also be some in National Archives, series M12).

## Potential difficulties

Not all towns are covered by public health records.

## USING HOSPITAL RECORDS

Many hospitals started with charitable endowments. An act of 1828 said that Justices of the Peace could build asylums with money from the rates; also from 1845 the parishes had to provide suitable accommodation for pauper lunatics.

### Where to find the records

◆ Original wills with endowments for hospitals, plus quarter sessions records showing when asylums were built, are usually at county record offices

◆ Hospital registers are usually at county record offices. You can search the National Archives records by hospital name to find if records for the hospital exist, for which dates, and which archives hold them

◆ Some hospitals keep their own records (e.g. St Bartholomew's in London and Addenbrooke's in Cambridge).

### Potential difficulties

Many records have been destroyed. Patients' records aren't released for 100 years or administrative records for 30 years.

## USING MANORIAL RECORDS

Manorial records are documents regarding the business dealings of manors. The manor was the basic unit of land ownership from feudal times; the lord of the manor was the most important resident. Manors varied in size; a parish could have more than one manor, or one manor might include several different towns.

Records exist from the mid 1200s (albeit patchy) up to 1925, when copyhold tenancies were abolished. The manor court rolls record the transfer of copyhold land between people, either by inheritance or by sale. There were four types of landholders:

- Freehold – freeholders had secure tenure and had no restrictions on their right to dispose of their lands
- Copyhold – copyholders were customary tenants. They held a 'copy' of the entry in the manor court roll which recorded them as tenants
- Leasehold – leaseholders held land that was leased for a specified time (often 21 years)
- Tenant at will – exactly as it sounds, tenants at will held their land at the will of the lord of the manor. They were often the poorest tenants.

Manors also had private courts, which controlled:

- The approval of tenancies
- Local customs and regulations
- Management and use of the land
- The behaviour of its tenants.

## What information they contain
Entries in the rolls contain:

- Descriptions of the property
- The names of the new and the previous tenant
- The date when the previous tenant was admitted
- Manorial court minutes.

## Where to find them
The Manorial Documents Register is held in the National Archives and shows where manorial records for England and Wales are held. The Welsh Manorial Documents Register and some of the English register can be searched online at the National Archives website (http://www.nationalarchives.gov.uk.mdr).

## Potential difficulties

Many have been lost. Before 1733 the records are usually in Latin. They also tend to be dated in regnal years (see Appendix 4), usually for Lady Day (25 March) and Michaelmas (29 September). Note that before 1752 New Year's Day was 25 March, so you need to be careful about the date (see Chapter 2, page 22, for more information about dates).

# 4

# Finding out about a building

This chapter covers the kind of evidence that you could use to help you find out more about a building: what information each sort of evidence contains, where to find it and where to go next, as well as highlighting potential difficulties with the evidence.

As with all local history, there are different strands to the history of the building:

- Original construction of and changes to the building itself
- Who lived there
- What the building was used for
- Any events that happened there.

The sources you use to find out information for one strand can help give you leads for a different strand, or confirm evidence you found in a different source.

With buildings, it is always best to do some general background research (using secondary sources), then start with the present and work back, switching between sources if necessary to follow the trail. The three main types of sources for researching the history of a building are:

- Physical sources
- Secondary sources
- Documentary sources.

## LOOKING AT PHYSICAL SOURCES

This is the building itself: what the building looks like now, and what it looked like in old sketches or photographs. This might help you see if any alterations were made and also help you date the physical changes. There are also tell-tale signs of alteration:

◆ Changes in the colour, shape, size and bonding (layout pattern) of bricks
◆ Windows – if they are symmetrical on one side and not on the other, the house may have been altered; blind windows may have been filled in to avoid window taxes
◆ Changes to the roofline
◆ The back door being moved
◆ Parts of the house obviously added on (particularly if they're not symmetrical changes).

### Dating the property

◆ Older buildings tend to be nearer the centre of a settlement and built with smaller bricks; however, older buildings are also more likely to have been rebuilt, and reclaimed materials might have been used during a rebuilding or addition. Original brickwork is most likely to be found in a cellar
◆ Check neighbouring buildings – are they of a similar style?
◆ Check architectural guides (such as the glossary in Pevsner) to help you date architectural features of the property
◆ Check the roofspace – the size of the beams can help you date the building
◆ Look at the number of and size of chimney stacks (this might help when looking at hearth tax assessments – but beware of 'false' chimneys which don't actually relate to a hearth in the building!)
◆ The building may have a date stone to give you some clues (but remember this may commemorate something other than the building of the property)

◆ Is the building listed? If so, it may be in the listings of the Department of the Environment; copies are available in your local library

◆ Check in which parish, manor or administration unit the building lics; this will help you later when you're checking maps and documentary sources (though remember that boundaries change over time).

## Looking at the building's past use

Buildings often change their use depending on the owner. So what's now a residential building might have been a barn, a mill, a shop, a pub, a school or a former religious building; and a shop might have once have been a house that was converted in the 17th century when its owner changed the layout of the ground floor for business and lived over the shop. You can also tell if a building was used for weaving, as there is usually a long row of windows on the top floor to let in the light. Mills used to have houses attached to them; the machinery or mill itself might no longer be there, but the millpond and stream might be.

Street directories (see Chapter 8) can help you find out what the building was used for in the past – though remember that house names and numbers change, as do street names, so you may need to cross-reference the information against other records (such as census returns and rate books) to confirm you are looking at the right building.

## Using photographic evidence

Taking a photograph of the building as it is now – close-ups of features, from different angles and including some of the environs – will be useful when comparing the present-day building against earlier photographs, plans or sketches. You may see some changes in the structure, or changes in the neighbouring buildings.

There may also be photographic or sketched evidence of the building and/or its environment in the past – your local library may have a photographic collection which may also be available online (and indexed by place/street/building name), or there may be books of old postcards or photographs published about your area which contain an image of the building you're studying. Again, they're useful for comparison with a modern photograph to help you identify changes.

### Using oral evidence

It's worth talking to former owners and neighbours, especially those who have lived in the area for a long time; they may remember previous inhabitants of the building or even previous uses. Be tactful about interviewing people (see Chapter 10) and check anecdotes against fact where possible.

Local historians may have done some research on the building already, so it's worth checking with your local group.

## LOOKING AT SECONDARY SOURCES
### Using Pevsner

*The Buildings of England* series by Nikolaus Pevsner is the classic architectural guide to buildings in each county, and there is a rolling programme of updates (so it's worth checking the previous edition as well as the latest one). The building you're looking at may be listed in some detail if it's architecturally significant.

*What information it contains*
There is an introductory overview of the area, covering:

◆ Topography
◆ Geology
◆ Building materials
◆ Different ages (e.g. prehistory, iron age/Roman, saxon/early medieval, conquest to Reformation, architecture from 1550–1700/ 1700–1830/Victorian/20th century

◆ Local architects

◆ Churches and furnishings.

Then there's a descriptive gazetteer arranged alphabetically by place. For a major city this is also within street order and the significant buildings are listed along with:

◆ A note of when it was built

◆ A description of the building

◆ Points of interest, such as which architect worked on restoration or alterations

◆ A brief historical note (e.g. the Norwich and North-East Norfolk edition refers to the Briton's Arms at 9 Elm Hill; it mentions that the building used to be a *béguinage* and was the only house in the street to survive the city fires in 1507).

Note that for towns and villages, only the significant buildings are listed – streets might not be.

There's also a glossary of architectural terms (which will help you spot features in the building you're studying), an index of artists, an index of patrons and residents mentioned, an index of places, and an index of streets and buildings in the listed city.

Copies should be available (either as reference or to borrow) at your local library; and they are also available in bookshops.

## Using street directories

Briefly, you may find information about significant buildings in the parish in the 'potted history' section before the street lists; the building you're studying, together with its occupant and trade, may also be listed in the street lists. In the directories before the 1890s, addresses don't tend to be given, so it is easiest to work backwards to make sure that you are looking at the right property. A directory listing can confirm what you have learned from title deeds and possibly give more information about the person who lived there, or provide an extra lead.

### Using the Victoria County History (VCH)
See Chapter 1, page 6 for more detail.

### Using the National Monuments record
This is held at by English Heritage at their public search rooms at Kemble Drive, Swindon SN2 2GZ. You can also check some of English Heritage databases online at www.english-heritage.org.uk – particularly good ones are Pastscape www.pastscape.org/ which contains descriptions of archaeological details, pictures, and links to maps and aerial photographs; and Images of England www.imagesofengland.org.uk/ which holds photographic records of listed buildings.

## LOOKING AT DOCUMENTARY SOURCES
For privately owned buildings, there are quite a few sources of documents. The most important ones, if you are trying to trace the history of a building, would be the property's title deeds (freehold or leasehold), as you will be able to work back through them to find out when the property changed hands. But if you don't have a complete set of deeds (or you are tracing the history of a building that doesn't belong to you), you may be able trace part of the history elsewhere. These include:

Documents of ownership and occupation:

◆ Title deeds of property (freehold or leasehold)
◆ Street directories (see above, page 87, and Chapter 8)
◆ Census returns
◆ Hearth tax assessments
◆ Land tax assessments.

Maps and images:

- Ordnance Survey maps (see Chapter 7)
- Valuation maps and schedules 1910–15 (aka 'Domesday', see Chapter 7)
- Tithe maps 1840–5 and apportionments (see Chapter 7)
- Enclosure award maps and schedules (see Chapter 7)
- Architectural drawings.

Changes to the building:

- Sales particulars
- Building control plans and planning applications
- Road order maps and deposited plans.

If the property was on Crown land, there is unlikely to be much material available. If there is a collection of papers relating to the estate at the local record office, it might contain deeds recording the purchase and disposal of land, leases to tenants (land, farms, houses), holdings and possibly maps.

For public buildings, you may not be able to access the title deeds. However, some of the sources listed above might yield information about the property's use and ownership, and there are additional resources that might tell you about the building and changes to it, including:

- Pevsner (see above, page 86)
- Department of Environment list
- National Monuments record centre maps

For churches, there are additional sources of information:

◆ Bishop's registers and visitation records
◆ Faculty court books (for changes made to the structure of churches)
◆ Consecration records and title deeds
◆ Parish records (see Chapter 3)
◆ Churchyard surveys.

There may also be websites for organisations which own specific buildings such as a theatre; a government website for a town hall; or for pubs (for example, in Norfolk we have Norfolk Pubs www.norfolk pubs.co.uk) and there's also the Pub History Society www.pubhistory society.co.uk/. County record offices hold licensing records for pubs.

## LOOKING AT DOCUMENTS OF OWNERSHIP AND OCCUPATION
### Using the title deeds of a property (freehold or leasehold)

Freehold property is when person A sells to person B. Between the 16th and 19th century there were two forms of conveyancing:

◆ Bargain and sale – where the owner of the property agrees to sell the property to the buyer at a set price
◆ Lease and release – where the owner leases the property to another person for a year, and then the day after the end of the lease there is a 'release', so the lessor (the owner) gives up the right to recover the property from the lessee (the person who leases the property but wants to buy it). Once the release was made, it was effectively the same as an ordinary bargain and sale.

There are also leaseholds, where the owner of the property (landlord) rents the property to someone else (tenant). Most leases were for:

- A year
- A term of years (usually 7 years or a multiple of 7 years)
- A term of lives (usually 3).

*What information they contain*
Freehold conveyances will show:

- The date
- The names of the seller and buyer
- The consideration (price paid)
- A clause defining the type of conveyance (bargain and sale or lease and release, as described above)
- A description of the property.

Leases will show:

- The date
- The names of the owner and lessee
- A description of property (often along the lines of 'hath sett to farm' or 'hath to farm let')
- The period of lease
- The annual rent
- Any 'reservations' to the landlord (often rights to woods or minerals on the land)
- Any 'covenants' (special conditions).

Deeds should give a short description of the property and its location; they will also give the names of former owners and occupiers. If there are abstracts of title, they may contain extracts from earlier deeds that have been lost. If there is an enfranchisement deed, this shows that the building once belonged to a manor (i.e. was copyhold) so there may be records of the building in the manor court rolls and books. Deeds tend to be kept in bundles so you should find a series of deeds for the same property in that bundle in an archive, but bundles are often broken up and sold.

*Where to find them*

If it is your house, you may have the deeds, or the deeds may be held by your mortgage company – check with your solicitor to see what's available.

*Potential difficulties*

Deeds tend to contain a lot of legal terms, so you need to a working knowledge of property law – note that they are often in Latin until the 16th century. Getting hold of the deeds themselves can be a problem, as they're often not indexed in record offices. When you do find them, they will need careful handling; they may be hard to unfold without damaging, so there will be a 'title' written on the back – that is, on the outside of the folded document – to identify it. The further back the deeds go, the harder you may find it to read the handwriting – so always work backwards.

## Using census returns

Census returns can help you see who occupied the building. Work backwards from 1901 census, and cross-reference the information you find against the other evidence you have. See Chapter 3, page 50.

You also need to be aware that if a property was unoccupied on census night, it will not be listed in the census; also that census returns name the occupier rather than the owner of the property, in which case the information might not tie up with the deeds.

## Using hearth tax assessments

See Chapter 3, page 58.

## Using land tax assessments
See Chapter 3, page 57.

# LOOKING AT MAPS AND IMAGES
As well as checking photographs, postcards and sketches (see above), it is also worth checking maps of different dates (see Chapter 7 for a fuller discussion of maps). You may be able to work out roughly when the building was first built, from when it first appears on a map; and, depending on the scale of the map, you might also be able to see whether the building changed in size and shape between maps of different dates, which will help you pin down alteration dates. Owner/occupier names are shown on some maps.

If the building existed before 1939 you should be able to find it on an Ordnance Survey map; if it existed before the first Ordnance Survey map for the area was made, you may find it on a tithe map; and you may also find its occupants in the census returns and rate books (see Chapter 3).

The most important thing with maps is to start with the latest Ordnance Survey map and work backwards. Note that the property may be shown on old county maps (for example, in Norfolk you'd look at Bryant or Greenwood), but any drawings tend to be of large properties only. Your local records office will be able to give you advice on sources of other maps.

## Using Ordnance Survey maps
They are available at the National Archives and county record offices. See Chapter 7, page 125.

## Using tithe maps
Under the Tithes Commutation Act of 1836, about three quarters of the parishes and towns in England and Wales were surveyed during the

1840s and tithe maps were produced of the areas, together with sched-ules listing every field and plot of land. See Chapter 7, page 120, for more information. The National Archives hold copies of each map and schedule; they are also available at county record offices and diocesan record offices.

### Using valuation maps

The map may contain a detailed plan of the building 1910–1915. Not all record offices hold copies of every single map in the area; although they are likely to have the valuation field books, without the map you won't know which building the plot number refers to. See Chapter 7, page 127.

### Using enclosure award maps

See Chapter 7, page 124.

### Using architectural drawings

Your county record office may have some collections of architects' drawings (particularly if they go along with building control plans and planning applications). There is also a collection of architects' drawings in the National Archive – see series NG 6 for workhouses, hospitals, museums, libraries, and town halls.

## LOOKING AT CHANGES TO THE BUILDING
### Using sales particulars

Many record offices contain catalogues of house sales/auctions; you may also see sales particulars listed in local newspapers. However, unless you know the date (within a couple of months) of the sale, you will end up searching a lot of documents with no guarantee that you will come across the information you're looking for.

*What information they contain*
These include:

◆ The auctioneer's name
◆ Date, time and place of auction
◆ Who instructed the sale (e.g. the personal representatives of the late Mr Smith)
◆ Details of the main building, its construction and any machinery and outbuildings included, plus a description of the land and its extent (in acres, roods and perches)
◆ Detailed description of a house – for example, on 14 June 1907 a sale of a mill complex at Beccles listed 'a Capital Brick, Plaster and Tiled Dwelling-House' and described the rooms as 'Dining Room, Drawing Room, Kitchen, two Pantries, Office and Five Bedrooms', as well as a garden and orchard.

*Where to find them*
As well as the sources mentioned above, if the building is sufficiently large, there may also be an adverisement in national newspapers, such as those in *The Times*; you can search the database of *The Times* 1785–1985 online.

## Using building control plans and planning applications
Since the late 1800s, local authorities have had to approve new build-ings and major alterations to existing buildings. To give approval, they need to see planning applications and this also has to be passed by the building control consultancy. Your county record office may have some collections of architects' drawings.

*What information they contain*
Planning applications often have architectural drawings and supporting papers for any application for alterations or new buildings.

*Where to find them*

Plans are held at your county record office, local building control or planning departments. However, note that few plans survive for buildings built before the late 19th century.

## Using road order maps and deposited plans

See Chapter 7, page 132.

## LOOKING AT SOURCES OF INFORMATION FOR PUBLIC BUILDINGS

### Using bishop's registers and visitation records

Bishop's registers give the record of the history of the church:

- When it was consecrated
- If anything (such as bells, church ornaments, organs or clocks) were presented, when and by whom
- If the church was united with another (e.g. during the Black Death when whole parishes died)
- Any consecrations of specific parts.

Visitation records reflect visits made to the parish churches by the bishop or archdeacon. Bishops were meant to visit every part of their diocese every three years, and archdeacons were meant to visit every part of their archdeaconry every year. They would ask ministers about their congregation and the physical state of the church, and the results would be recorded in comperta books (i.e. books of 'things discovered' during the visit).

*Looking at the information they contain*

Bishop's Registers

- Records of any institutions to benefices (i.e. the ecclesiastical living) made by the bishop, including the date of institutions, the names of the clergyman and patron, and details of the benefice

♦ Copies of earlier documents such as:
  - Appropriations (i.e. transfers of parish tithes to a religious institution)
  - Presentations
  - Advowsons (the right to appoint the priest – this belonged to the person who built the church, and was granted in the 12th or 13th century to a religious house)
  - Unions with other parishes
  - Consolidation of benefices
  - Church consecrations.

You should also be able to see in the registers when the parish church was first built and to which saint or saints it was dedicated.

Visitation records
These were basically a record of the condition of the church building.

*Where to find them*
These can be found at the county record office.

## Using faculty court books

If a church building needed to be altered or pulled down, the bishop granted a faculty. The faculties were recorded in the faculty court books; there may also be faculty petitions (e.g. if someone contested a faculty relating to a tomb, pew or memorial), which were dealt with in the bishop's Consistory Court. When the faculty was granted, a bond would be given to carry out the work; there would also be accounts for work completed. After 1940, an archdeacon's certificate was required to say that the work had been completed in accordance with the faculty.

*What information they contain*
Faculties deal with repairs, alterations and removal/destruction: for example, bells, pews, the removal of lead from the church roof.

*Where to find them*

These can be found at the county record office.

## Using consecration records and title deeds

Consecration registers survive from around the 18th century and record the bishop's consecration of:

◆ Churches
◆ Chapels
◆ Mission halls
◆ Burial grounds.

The papers of the consecrations themselves sometimes include the title deeds and a plan of the site.

There are also diocesan deeds and augmentation deeds (i.e. from when the monasteries were dissolved in the 1530s – what the Crown did with seized lands).

*Where to find them*

These can be found at the county record office, local diocesan office and National Archives.

## Using glebe terriers

Glebe terriers are the survey of church property in a parish; they list houses, fields and sometimes tithes.

*What information they contain*

◆ A description of the churchyard (which can be compared with the tithe maps)
◆ A list of the church furnishings such as books, vestments and bells
◆ A description of church property (e.g. houses) and tenants' names.

*Where to find them*
These can be found at the county record office or diocesan office; some have also been published by local record societies.

## Using parish records
As well as the registers of births, marriages and burials, parish records contain information about the church and any repairs made to it. The rector was responsible for the upkeep of the chancel, and the church-wardens were responsible for upkeep of the nave and tower.

*What information they contain*
- Benefice papers
- Churchwardens' accounts – record of amounts spent on the mainte-nance of the church
- Vestry minutes – information about alteration and repair work
- Sequestration accounts – when an ecclesiastical living became vacant, a sequestrator was responsible for the chancel and its upkeep.

*Where to find them*
These can be found at the county record office.

*Potential difficulties*
The survival is patchy and varies between parishes; you are unlikely to find them before the 1500s.

## Using churchyard surveys
Churchyards have been surveyed by people interested in churchyards; for example, in Norfolk the WI made several surveys in the 1980s.

Also, sometimes when permission was granted to move stones the local authority made copy of the inscriptions and deposited them with the Registrar General.

*What information they contain*
- Plan of the churchyard
- Inscriptions on gravestones and memorials.

*Where to find them*
County record office. Some transcriptions (for stones moved) are at the National Archives in series RG37; others are with the local branch of the Society of Genealogists.

*Potential difficulties*
Gravestones get harder to read every year due to weathering, pollution and vandalism, and some may be illegible. Churchyards in cities are often built over.

## Using cartularies
Monastic charters confirmed that a religious house had the right to possess its lands. Although many documents were destroyed during the dissolution of the monasteries in the 1530s, the charters were to do with the legal history of the estates, so they were often used by the new owners. The charters were written up in books known as cartularies.

*What information they contain*
- Boundaries
- Field names
- Information about local families and tenants.

*Where to find them*
These can be found at county record offices.

## LOOKING AT LISTED BUILDINGS
Department of Environment lists are published for each local authority area and contain short historical and architectural descriptions of the buildings. These lists should be available in local libraries.

- Grade I – buildings of national importance or of exceptional interest
- Grade II* – particularly important buildings of more than special interest
- Grade II – buildings of special interest that need preservation (roughly 93% of listed buildings fall into this category).

## PUTTING IT INTO PRACTICE

In practice, you'll need two files: one for the building itself and its appearance and interior, and one for its occupants/owners/any events that happened. Some of the sources will have a bearing on both strands. Bear in mind that house names and street names change – and there also might have been a different building previously on the same site.

### Tracing the building itself

Start with the maps and see whether the building appears there:

- Ordnance Survey maps (work backwards as far as you can)
- 1910 maps and hereditaments
- Tithe maps and awards
- Enclosure maps and apportionments.

Note the details of:

- The building
- Its owners – names, ages, occupations etc. (you can use these as leads for tracing the inhabitants).

If it is a specialist building (such as a church or chapel, listed building, school, former workhouse or hospital), check the Department of Environment registers.

Look at the deeds – if you can trace the date of any sale, see if sale particulars exist at the county record office or if there is something listed in the local newspaper. If the sale is recent there may be files at the estate agency; if the sale is in the 19th century or before, there tend to be very rich details in advertisements in the local newspaper. This may include a description of the building, and even outbuildings or part of the structure that no longer exists. Also check for any mention in the Victoria County History, the street directories' 'potted history' and in any standard county history.

For specialist buildings (such as schools, hospitals), there may be registers available. If you know the rough date of when it was built or altered, it will narrow down your search in local newspapers. Newspaper reports may give you more detail about who originally owned the land or gave donations to a building fund.

For the 19th century and earlier it is often useful to start with the names listed in the tithe apportionment and then to move backwards to the land tax returns, 1780–1832, and rate books (e.g. the Poor Rate). Bear in mind that descriptions of property in the rate books are often very sketchy. It becomes easier if the owner's names in the tithe apportionment are the same as those in the last available rate book. You can then move backwards by rental value (and the position of the property in the book, which usually reflects the collector's route!). A change in rental value may reflect alterations or additions to the house.

### Tracing the owner/occupier of the building

Start with the deeds and work back as far as you can. The Land Registry will also have some details of current and former owners. Cross-reference these against details from the 1910 maps, the tithe map and enclosure map (see Chapter 7); this may help fill in the gaps.

If the person occupying the building carried on a trade, you may be able to trace them through the street directories (see Chapter 8); but remember that the house name/number may change between directories or might not even be listed.

Check census returns (see Chapter 3) and cross-reference them against the other evidence you have. Work backwards from 1901 census – you may be able to trace back generations of occupiers if the house (or tenancy) was handed down through a family. Remember that street names tend to change over the years.

See Chapter 3, 'Finding a Person', for information about tracing a trail backwards.

**Tracing events at the building**
With specialist buildings (such as schools, workhouses or hospitals), if you know rough dates of events (such as the opening of the building, expansion, moves elsewhere or an epidemic), it will narrow down your search in local newspapers and you can see how the area was affected.

With any building, you should be able to trace events such as fires, floods, accidents, or criminal cases via indexes to the local newspapers (if available), through annals, or through secondary sources. Once you've narrowed down the date, you can look it up in the newspaper and then maybe trace from there through to court records or minutes. For example, I knew from secondary sources that in Norwich there was a severe flood in August 1912, so I could pin down the date fairly quickly in the local newspapers and that gave me leads to follow up about which streets were most affected.

I also discovered in Mackie's *Annals* that in January 1827 there was an incident with a bull at the Bess O'Bedlam pub in Oak Street, and was able to trace that back to the original report in the *Norfolk Chronicle*. The report told me that the bull managed to get up the stairs and interrupted a musical party, and 'the animal was dislodged with great difficulty'.

Chapter 5 gives more information about tracing events.

# 5

# Finding Out About an Event

This chapter covers the kind of evidence that you could use to help you find out more about an event – what information each sort of evidence contains, where to find it and where to go next, as well as highlighting potential difficulties with the evidence:

◆ Using eyewitness accounts (newspaper reports, letters, diaries, scrapbooks, oral history, trial records, company/institution records, court records)
◆ Using secondary sources (annals, other historians' work).

To begin with, do you want to know more about a specific event, or do you want to know more about things that happened in a particular parish, street or building over a period of time? Or you might be looking at a group of events, such as changes in a trade or industry.

If it's a specific event, it is likely that you already know the approximate date and can go straight to primary sources – records and eyewitness accounts, as well as newspaper reports.

If you're looking at what happened over a period of time, or are looking for a specific group of events (such as riots, crime, fires, entertainment, politics) you need to try to narrow your search a little first, which means using secondary sources to pin down the dates of the events you're looking at.

## LOOKING AT EYEWITNESS ACCOUNTS

Eyewitness accounts are contemporary records of events, made during the events themselves or maybe later. These include:

◆ Local newspaper reports – often (and particularly for 19th-century trial reports) these include direct quotes from the people involved in an event and may be a verbatim record

◆ Letters – they may have accounts from someone who was involved in the event

◆ Diaries and notebooks – again, this may be an account from someone who was there and may quote people and give accounts of events. For example, in Norfolk we have the diaries of Parson Woodforde. Some county record societies publish these records: for example, Norfolk Record Society published *The Notebook of Robert Doughty 1662–1665*. Doughty was a Justice of the Peace and the records made in his notebook give rich details about life in the North Walsham area during the period

◆ Scrapbooks – these were often made in the 19th century and include newspaper cuttings, postcards, handbills, broadsheets, engravings and pamphlets; although in some sense this is a 'secondary' source (particularly if the person who compiled the scrapbook copied out reports in longhand rather than clipping the newspaper cutting and pasting it into a book). There may also be annotations and comments from the person who compiled the scrapbook

◆ Handbills

◆ Broadsheets (particularly from public executions)

◆ Pamphlets – may have been written at the time or shortly afterwards

◆ Court records – mayor's court, quarter sessions, assizes, consistory courts

◆ Official log books – such as school log books (which may be detailed), prison registers, Bridewell registers, surgeon's reports

◆ Minutes of meetings.

## Looking at the information they contain

◆ Newspaper reports (local and national) – will generally follow the reporter's creed of 'who, what, when, where, why and how'. They may include direct quotes from people involved in an event; they may also include comments from the reporter linking the event with other local events (e.g. in an opinion piece). This will give you other leads to follow up.

◆ Letters – anything and everything!

◆ Diaries and notebooks – depends on the diarist. For example, in *The Notebook of Robert Doughty 1662–1665*, he talks about issuing a warrant of the peace on 5 July 1664 against Mary Shale 'upon the oath of Robert Colker (labourer) of [Paston], whom she threat [sic] to knock on the head'. The Shales must have been a bit of a thorn in his side, because later that same month he had to issue another warrant against Mary, this time because she threatened to knock Margaret Empson and her children on the head! A couple of months previously, her husband had been suspected of stealing a lamb, selling it and pocketing the proceeds

◆ Scrapbooks – depends on the interests of the person who compiled the scrapbook, but these could include cuttings from magazines and newspapers about a particular area or family, plus photographs or sketches

◆ Handbills – often advertising people's wares

◆ Broadsheets (from public executions) – often headed as an 'account of the trial, execution, life, character and behaviour of the person executed. They usually contained:

  – The name of the accused with the place and date of execution

  – The reason he or she had been indicted

  – An account of the trial (e.g. if it was particularly long or crowded)

  – The evidence against the prisoner (i.e. what happened) – sometimes (e.g. in the case of the 'Hempnall Poisoner' Charles Daines) this will include verbatim comments of witnesses in the trial (which can be corroborated against newspaper reports as well as in the assizes records)

- Sometimes a 'moral' or comments on the case or a religious text that the printer thought appropriate
- Sometimes a character description (may include the age and occupation of the accused)
- The confession of the accused
- Details of the execution (e.g. the number of people who attended it – the broadsheet of Samuel Yarham's execution in 1846 printed by Walker and Co of Church Street St Miles, Norwich, states 'No execution of late years had attracted so large an assemblage of spectators, some thousands being present')
- Printer's name and address
- Sometimes a woodcut showing either the crime or the execution
◆ Pamphlets – could be absolutely anything, from rules and regulations to an account of a local event
◆ Court records – mayor's court, quarter sessions, assizes, consistory courts (see Chapter 3)
◆ Official log books – such as school log books (which may be detailed), prison registers, Bridewell registers, surgeon's reports (see Chapter 3)
◆ Minutes – usually the time, date and place of meeting, who attended, business discussed and 'any other business'.

### Finding them
Local studies centres are the best place to start – the librarians can advise where collections are held.

◆ Newspaper reports – generally in the local studies centre or local record office; some may be available online; also at the British Library in Colindale. You can also search *The Times* online digital archives 1785–1985. For example, if you wanted to look up a case which made national headlines such the Stanfield Hall murders in Norfolk (where James Blomfield Rush was executed for the murder of Isaac Jermy, the Norwich recorder), you can look it up. You can also limit the search by date and by section (advertising, business, editorial. features, news, people, picture gallery). The abstracts of the articles tell you:

- – The number of results (and lists them in date order)
- – The title of the article
- – Which section it's in
- – The byline of the reporter
- – The date, page, issue no. and column
- – How many words are in the section.

For example, the first abstract about the Stanfield Hall murders was for an article titled 'The Stanfield-Hall Murders', in the news section. The byline was 'From our own reporter'; it appeared in The Times on Tuesday, Dec 05, 1848, page 5, column E; the issue number was 20038; and it was 975 words long. When you look at the article itself, your search term(s) are highlighted, so it's easy to scan.

- ◆ Letters – the originals may be in the local record office; the local record society may have published some letters and these publications may be available for reference in your local studies centre (or on the second-hand book market)
- ◆ Diaries – the originals may be in the local record office; as with letters, the local record society may have published some diaries and these publications may be available for reference in your local studies centre (or on the second-hand book market)
- ◆ Scrapbooks – the originals are likely to be in the local studies centre or local record office
- ◆ Handbills – generally in local studies centre or local record office
- ◆ Broadsheets (from public executions) – generally in local studies centre or local record office
- ◆ Pamphlets – generally in local studies centre or local record office
- ◆ Court records – mayor's court, quarter sessions, assizes, consistory courts – either local record office or National Archives, or possibly local ecclesiastical archives

◆ Official log books – such as school log books (which may be detailed), prison registers, Bridewell registers, surgeon's reports – some in the National Archives, others in the local record office

◆ Minutes – generally in the local record office.

## Avoiding the potential difficulties

◆ Newspaper reports may reflect the political bias or attitude of a particular newspaper; for example, the trial reports in the *Norwich Mercury* are far more sensationalist than those in the *Norfolk Chronicle and Norwich Gazette*. Copies may not be available, as survival of earlier newspapers is patchy; there may also be copyright issues (see Chapter 9)

◆ Letters – there may be copyright issues and if the letters are held in a special collection you may need to get permission before you can access them. Reading the handwriting of originals becomes progressively more difficult as you go back through the archives; you may need to make yourself an alphabet to help you decipher difficult words, based on letter formations in words you know for definite.

◆ Diaries – as with letters, there are copyright, access and handwriting issues. You also need to be sure whether the diaries are authentic. Were they written at the time of the events described, or retrospectively? Are they telling the truth or glossing over/sexing up parts?

◆ Scrapbooks – may not contain info you are looking for

◆ Handbills – survival is patchy

◆ Broadsheets (from public executions) – survival is patchy; also, the printer may have made up some of the story or embellished it to sell more copies

◆ Pamphlets – survival may be patchy; as with letters and diaries, there may be copyright and access issues

◆ Court records – some may not be available; the records might not be indexed so you will have to search through documents of little relevance (so it's worth trying the online search engine at National Archives);

some records may be in Latin (particularly consistory court records before 1733 – consistory courts deal with cases following visitations, damage to church property and misappropriation of church goods)

◆ Official log books – amount of details vary; records may not be complete; and there may be handwriting issues as detailed above

◆ Minutes – survival may be patchy.

# LOOKING AT SECONDARY SOURCES
## Using annals

A good start would be 'annals' – particularly in Victorian times, antiquarians tended to set themselves a task of working through past editions of newspapers and noting the major events. Sometimes this is in index form; sometimes more details are given. For example, in Norfolk Charles Mackie prepared annals from the *Norfolk Chronicle* from 1801–99 to produce two volumes giving very brief details of events. When I was researching *Norwich: Street by Street*, I found the annals useful as a starting point because it saved me searching through every single newspaper to find the major events in the city during those years.

*What information they contain*

Annals tend to focus on local rather than national news, although they may make mention of coronations and election of prime ministers. The kind of things you can expect to see mentioned are:

◆ Local extreme weather events – such as floods, earthquakes, fireballs

◆ Politics – local election campaigns, who stood and the electoral returns; election of mayors

◆ Local tragedies – fires, accidents, houses falling down, wartime air raids

◆ Entertainments – details of advertisements for exhibitions at halls and pubs (for example, in Norwich in 1815, Monsieur du Pain did a show at the Angel Hotel where he immersed his feet in boiling lead); circuses and menageries (and occasionally what was exhibited (for

example, in Norwich in 1823 Drake's Menagerie included a perform-
ing elephant, a boa constrictor and a live sea serpent measuring
'more than 300 feet in length'); and shows (for example, in July
1831, Paganini played at the Corn Exchange in Norwich)

◆ New buildings and inventions (for example, in 1818 the hatter and
hosier business of Joseph Oxley & sons was the first to introduce
gaslight into a Norwich factory)

◆ Brief obituaries of local worthies (often a philanthropist, owner of a
large business, mayor or surgeon)

◆ Brief mentions of crimes (embezzlements as well as murders)

◆ Hoaxes (for example, in 1823, Mrs Chestnut of St Giles advertised
that she was going to exhibit a 'machine exemplifying perpetual
motion', saying that it 'has been going since it was invented, upwards
of 7 years'; the Mayor was suspicious, investigated it and banned it
as a fake)

◆ Unusual funerals

◆ Sensationalist cases (for example, in Norwich in July 1838 the case
of George Perowne, a local vet who'd made a bargain with his
employee to buy his body and cut it up for scientific investigation,
and the wife of the deceased claimed he was a body-stealer).

*Where to find them*

Local studies centres are the best place to start – the librarians can
advise you if any annals exist for your area. Copies might be available
at county record offices, too.

*Where to go next*

Once you have pinned down a date (even if it's approximate), you will be
able to go to the newspapers for fuller details. If you are interested in crime,
then having the date of an execution will give you a rough date of the trial,
so you can look up the trial records. (It's also worth checking newspaper
reports for 19th-century trials as they were very detailed at that time.)

*Potential difficulties*

The compiler of the annals may have interests that aren't relevant to your research. For example, Mackie focused heavily on local elections but ignored quite a few crimes and major fires, so when I looked through various newspapers I found stories he'd ignored but which were perfect for my research.

Newspapers all have their particular bias, so you may get a different version of the story if you check with a different newspaper or different source.

## Using indexes to newspapers

If there are no annals available for the years you're interested in, it's also possible that a previous researcher or local studies student has indexed some of the newspapers.

See Chapter 9.

## Using other historians' work

Whether it is a modern survey of the county's history, an ancient survey or a monograph about a particular parish or street, you may find mentions of the event you're researching. Better still, there may be footnotes or references to other material within books, pamphlets and monographs that will give even more information about the event you're researching, or maybe a different viewpoint. Local studies centres are the best place to start; the librarians can advise.

*Potential difficulties*

How accurate are the details? Can you trust the translations in the book (particularly of Latin documents)? Has the author copied someone else's mistakes? Some of these questions can be answered by articles in antiquarian papers – for example, the historian Walter Rye notes that some sources of Norwich history are more reliable than others, and gives examples of poor translations or mistakes to back up his views.

Interpretation of events can also change over time. For example, when I was researching *Norwich: Stories of a City* I found that Robert Kett was treated as a traitor in 1549; the chronicler Holinshed calls his followers 'wicked caitiffs' and the contemporary historian Sotherton claims that the rebels looted shops and warehouses, and made the citizens bake them bread and pasties to stop them looting the rest of their goods. Contemporary city records are just as scathing, saying that the Earl of Warwick delivered the city from Kett and his rebels and decreed that every 27th of August the shops in the city should be shut and all citizens should go to their parish church when the bells rang at 7 a.m., and pray to God and for the king in remembrance of their deliverance – a practice that continued even as late as 1748. But by the mid-20th century, Kett was recognised as a hero who stood up for the rights of the common man against rack rents and enclosures, and in 1949, the citizens of Norwich placed a tablet on the Castle 'in reparation and honour to a notable and courageous leader in the long struggle of the common people of England to escape from a servile life into the freedom of just conditions'. Villain, hero, martyr? It all depends on which source you use – and what you choose to include in your account of events.

$$\textbf{6}$$

# Searching for Resources

This chapter covers where to find the evidence you need for your research – the different organisations that can help and the kind of material each organisation is likely to have.

The preceding chapters cover the kind of material available in the National Archives and county record office collections – and there are also online catalogues available to give you an idea of each archive's holdings at Access to Archive www.a2a.org.uk. So, rather than repeat that information, this section covers other kinds of archives.

There are also other specialist archives available, such as advertising, business, schools and hospitals; the best place to look up details for these is at the National Archives website, as you're able to search for specialist repositories by keyword searching. The website address is www.nationalarchives.gov.uk/archon/.

## FINDING FILM ARCHIVES

**British Film Institute, National Film and Television Archive**
21 Stephen Street
London
W1 1LN
Tel: 020 7957 4726
Website: www.bfi.org.uk

**East Anglian Film Archive**
The Archive Centre
Martineau Lane
Norwich
NR1 2DQ
Tel: 01603 592664
Website: www.uea.ac.uk/eafa/

**National Media Museum**
Bradford
West Yorkshire
BD1 1NQ
Tel: 0870 7010200
Website: www.nationalmedia
museum.org.uk

**Northern Region Film and Television Archive**
School of Arts and Media
University of Teesside
Middlesbrough
Tees Valley
TS1 3BA

Also c/o:

**Tyne & Wear Archive Service**
Blandford House
Blandford Square
Newcastle Upon Tyne
NE1 4JA
Tel: 0191 277 2250
Website: www.nrfta.org.uk/

**North West Film Archive**
Manchester Metropolitan University
Minshull House
47-49 Chorlton Street
Manchester
M1 3EU
Tel: 0161 2473097
Website: www.nwfa.mmu.ac.uk

**Pathe News**
British Pathe plc
c/o ITN Source
200 Gray's Inn Road
London
WC1X 8XZ
Tel:  0207 430 4480
Website: www.britishpathe.com/

**Screen Archive South East**
University of Brighton Grand
Parade
Brighton
BN2 0JY
Tel: 01273 643213
Website: www.brighton.ac.uk/
screenarchive/

**South West Film and Television
Archive**
Melville Building
Royal William Yard
Stonehouse
Plymouth
PL1 3RP
Tel: 01752 202650
Website: www.tswfta.co.uk

**Yorkshire Film Archive**
York St John University
Lord Mayor's Walk
York
YO31 7EX
Tel: 01904 716550
Website: www.yorkshirfilm
archive.com

# FINDING SOUND ARCHIVES

**British Library Sound Archive**
96 Euston Road
London
NW1 2DB
Tel: 020 7412 7676
Website:
www.bl.uk/collections/nsa

**Imperial War Museum Sound
Archive**
Correspondence Address:
Lambeth Road
London
SE1 6HZ
Tel: 020 7416 5363
Website:
http://collections.iwm.org.uk/serv
er/show/nav.00g007

**National Army Museum**
Department of Archives,
Photographs, Film and Sound
Royal Hospital Road
Chelsea
London
SW3 4HT
Tel: 020 7730 0717
Website: www.national-
army-museum.ac.uk

**National Screen and Sound Archive of Wales**
The National Library of Wales
Aberystwyth
SY23 3BU
Tel: 01970 632828
Website:
www.screenandsound.llgc.org.uk/

**North West Sound Archive**
Old Steward's Office
Clitheroe Castle
Clitheroe
Lancashire
BB7 1AZ
Tel: 01200 427897
Website:
www.gmcro.co.uk/other/NWSA/n
wsa.htm

**Wessex Film and Sound Archive**
Wessex Film and Sound Archive
Hampshire Record Office
Sussex Street
Winchester
SO23 8TH
Tel: 01962 847742
Website:
www.hants.gov.uk/record-
office/film

## FINDING OTHER ARCHIVE RESOURCES

**Society of Genealogists**
14 Charterhouse Buildings
Goswell Road
London
EC1M 4BA
Website: www.sog.org.uk

**Federation of Family History Societies**
Can put you in touch with your local society.
Website: www.ffhs.org.uk/

**Family History Centres (Church of Jesus Christ of Latter Day Saints)**
Can put you in touch with your nearest centre.
Family History Centre Library
64–8 Exhibition road
South Kensington
London
SW7 2PA
Tel: 0207 589 8561
Website: www.familysearch.org

# ⑦

# Using Maps

Before you look at a map, think about why the map was produced and by whom. What was it used for? Bear in mind that it might omit irrelevant details, or include deliberately false details for propaganda purposes, or it might even be a copy of an earlier map and not reflect the time when it was drawn.

There are some non-cartographic details which can help you look at this, such as:

- The title of the map (this will tell you what you are looking at, where and when it was produced)
- The scale
- The key (particularly if colours are used, and symbols, particularly ones less likely to be found in modern maps such as windmills, river crossings, turnpikes)
- The orientation of the map – usually the north is at the top, but it is worth checking if there is a compass rose in one corner
- Decoration around the edges of the map – this might include subscribers' names or even pictures of important buildings in the area.

If the key to the map is missing and you are unsure what the symbols or colours mean, ask the record office staff to help you. It may also be worth looking at other maps, made by the same cartographer in the same period, which might show a key.

It is also worth checking if there are other relevant maps you can use for comparison purposes – either ones made at a different date, or ones of a neighbouring property so you can check boundaries.

As well as using maps to trace changes in the use and ownership of an area, comparing maps from different eras can help you build up a fuller picture of a location.

You need to be aware of copyright law (especially if you're considering publishing your material). Maps that are less than 50 years old are still in copyright. You may be able to copy one A4 segment for your personal use, but check with the library or archive staff first. You may also need to sign a copyright declaration form and have your photocopy stamped.

Some maps may be too large or fragile to be copied on an A3 or plan copier – particularly older maps. You may be able to photograph the maps (check with archive staff), or perhaps a facsimile or digitised version may be available. Tracing is another possibility, though you will need to use clear plastic film between the map and the tracing paper to avoid damaging the map.

In all cases, if you are looking to publish any section of a map, always check with the archive staff. They will advise you if copyright permission is needed and how to get it.

## LOOKING AT THE DIFFERENT TYPES OF MAPS
### Using tithe maps

In England, a 'tithe' was paid to the church from early medieval times. The tithe itself was a tenth of the produce of the land – hay, wool, corn and the like. A third of the tithe (known as the 'small tithe') went to the vicar or deputy who served the church, and the remainder (known as the 'great tithe') went to the rector or the religious house that ruled the church. The tithe was meant to pay for the living of the parish priest.

After the dissolution of the monasteries, the rights to tithes passed into private hands. When lands were enclosed, tithe owners were often given allotments of land in compensation. Tithe owners (including churches) might also agree to exchange a payment in kind for a cash payment – this was known as commutation.

In 1836, the Tithe Commutation Act converted the tithe from a payment in kind to a 'rent charge'. The actual amount of the rent charge varied; it depended on the way the land was cultivated and the price of corn. The Tithe Commission was set up in London and sent assistant commissioners to implement the act in England and Wales; this was done between 1836 and about 1850. In order to work out the award, the commissioners had to commission surveys of the land, meet with the landowners and tithe owners, and draw up a provisional agreement of the charge; if there was disagreement, the commissioners would have to arbitrate and work out an award. Once the agreement or award was confirmed, one copy was kept in the parish chest, one was given to the bishop of the diocese, and one remained with the Tithe Commission. As part of the survey work, tithe maps were made.

*What information they contain*

The scale of the maps was between 12 and 25 inches to the mile, and the maps cover the whole parish. They show:

- Boundaries (including early medieval parish boundaries, tithe-free monastic land and areas not yet enclosed; also field boundaries with hedges, fences, stiles and gates)
- Buildings (inhabited ones such as farmhouses and cottages are red and other structures are marked in grey)
- Place names.

And possibly also, depending on who made the map:

♦ Roads, turnpikes and tollhouses
♦ Rivers, ponds and other bodies of water
♦ Railway lines
♦ Mills, factories, quarries, chalk pits and mines
♦ Woodlands
♦ Icehouses, dovecotes and lighthouses.

There was a full written schedule (or 'apportionment') with each map, describing the land, and field names were sometimes included. The schedule was arranged in alphabetic order of the landowner, and tenants are listed alphabetically underneath the landowner's name. Institutes (such as a turnpike trust, a chapel trustee and the parish) are listed at the end of the schedule. The apportionments generally show:

♦ Summary information of the parish: total area, name of tithe owner(s), acreage of titheable and non-titheable lands (and information about lands that were exempt from tithes)
♦ Name of landowner (first and surname)
♦ Name of occupier (first and surname: may be 'himself' if the occupier is also the landowner, and in some cases the very tantalising comment 'and others' – particularly for tenants)
♦ Plot number (you can match this to the map)
♦ Name and description of land and premises (this includes fields names, which are not shown on Ordnance Survey maps)
♦ State of cultivation (e.g. arable, pasture, rough grazing, marshland, timber, orchard, garden, hop field, market garden, meadow, coppice, paddock; however the type of crop isn't always shown, nor the type of livestock)
♦ Extent of land (in acres, roods and perches – there were 40 perches in a rood, and 4 roods in an acre. See Appendix 7 for more details about measures.)

- ◆ Amount of rent charge payable
- ◆ Remarks (e.g. if the plots became 'altered apportionments', usually when a railway was built)
- ◆ Summary of schedule listing the landowners in alphabetical order, occupiers (in order of amount of land held), total of rent charge from each owner to each tithe owner.

*Where to find them*

There is a complete set of tithe maps at the National Archives in section IR30 and apportionments in IR29; you should also find the diocesan and/or parish copy of the maps at your local record office. All of the Welsh apportionments and most of the English ones are in microform. There is also some correspondence and copies of reports in section IR18.

*Potential difficulties*

The parcel numbers of the land are not arranged numerically in the schedule, so you will have to look through the book to find the number.

Although they survive for almost all parishes, the maps vary in size, scale and accuracy – some give only the basics whereas others are much more detailed. Some of the maps are 14 feet square – they come in a roll, so you will need to book a map table at the record office to look at them and also use weights to hold them open. Any amendments will be shown on a linen-backed Ordnance Survey map (usually the 6-inch format).

The apportionment books are usually rolled up inside the tithe map (along with the amendments) and again you'll need to use weights to hold the pages where you want them.

The maps and apportionments are too large to copy on an A3 photocopier; as the books bound and fairly fragile, you won't be able to copy them on a plan-printer either. Alternatives are photographing the books/map (though this depends on your record office's policies) or transcribing it onto a photocopy of a 6-inch Ordnance Survey map.

## Using enclosure maps and awards

Until the 18th century, cultivation of land was based on the 'open field' system, where people had strips in each field and rights over common pasture and woodlands – 'common' land was actually owned privately, but people had 'rights of common' so they could let their animals graze over it.

Enclosure was where these open fields and commons were converted to individual plots of private land, often with a fence or hedge put round it to separate it from a neighbour's land. The first agreements were made privately, between a landowner and tenants; later, they were subject to an Act of Parliament.

Sometimes common land was divided between freeholders in a manor, and sometimes arable land was rearranged so that farmers who had strips of land in different large open fields would have a single larger piece of land instead. These plots were called 'allotments' and they ranged in size from a small parcel to several hundred acres.

From the 1780s onwards, a map of the land was included in an enclosure award. The clerk of the peace collected the awards before 1792; after that, the awards had to be included ('enrolled') in records of the quarter sessions. There were also notifications in the local newspapers.

The Enclosure Commission was established in 1845; after then, a central government department held a copy of all enclosure awards. The enclosure procedure also changed; instead of needing an individual Act of Parliament for each enclosure, people simply applied to the Commission. The Commission assessed all the applications once a year and, if they were successful, they were actioned together.

*What information they contain*

The enclosure maps vary; some show a map of the entire parish with its existing layout, and the proposals for enclosure superimposed on it. Sometimes it shows land ownership, roads, footpaths and boundaries. It may show who owned land, who bought it and how the land was affected by enclosure. Usually the maps come with a schedule; the number on each plot of land matches the number on the schedule, which will give the landowner's name, extent of holdings and the nature of tenure (freehold or copyhold). The schedule may also list rights of way and say who was responsible for maintaining boundaries.

*Where to find them*

These can be found in local record offices; for enclosures after 1845, the National Archives series MAF1. There is also correspondence about enclosures (including information about disputes) in series MAF25.

*Potential difficulties*

Not all parishes have enclosure maps. The maps may not cover the entire parish. Remember that 'enclosure' is also spelt 'inclosure' in some areas, when looking up the records.

## Using Ordnance Survey maps

The Ordnance Survey was established in 1791. Its function was to produce maps of Kent, Surrey and Sussex to help the military commanders prepare to repel French invaders. The first official map was produced in 1801.

After the war with France ended in 1815, the Board of Ordnance continued and expanded to the rest of the country. Although Christopher and John Greenwood started publishing 1-inch county maps in the 1820s, they abandoned the project when the Ordnance Survey project developed.

There were several editions:

◆ Old Series (completed 1870)
◆ Second edition (also known as the 'New Series', started in 1870)
◆ Third edition (revision of the 6-inch and 25-inch maps) for some areas in 1900 and 1920
◆ Fourth edition for some areas just before the Second World War.

If you compare different editions of Ordnance Survey maps for the same area, it will give you a picture of how that area has developed over time.

*What information they contain*
The Old Series were 1-inch maps (i.e. the scale was 1 inch to the mile) and the maps are basically a survey of the land,

The Second Edition had three different scales: 1 inch (i.e. one inch to the mile), 6 inches (i.e. six inches to the mile) and 25 inches (i.e. extremely detailed, twenty-five inches to the mile – this tends to be London and the larger towns). The 25-inch map shows railway lines, the shape and size of buildings, boundaries of fields and acreage sizes; it may also give house names, show the garden layout (including ponds), the number of seats in churches, the position of pillar boxes, lamp-posts and horse troughs, and the width of pavements.

*Where to find them*
Most libraries and record office have copies of the 1-inch maps. There are excellent collections at the National Archives and the British Library. You can see the 6-inch editions online on the Old Maps website www.old-maps.co.uk. There may also be some earlier maps online, depending on your county's archive; for example, Norfolk has various maps (including aerial photography) at www.historic-maps. norfolk.gov.uk/.

*Potential difficulties*

The Old Series maps tended to become out of date very quickly due to the expansion of the railway network and the way towns grew in the 19th century. Scales of maps less than the 25-inch map don't show railway lines at the correct width.

## Using Field Office Valuations ('Domesday' maps)

The Finance Act 1910 levied new duties on land, including 'increment value duty'; this was 20% of the increase on the site value of land at its valuation on 20 April 1909 and its sale at a later date. People were exempt if the land was farmland with no greater value than its current agricultural value, or houses with land that was less than 50 acres and worth less than £75 per acre. The 'increment value duty' was repealed in 1920 but the Valuation Office made surveys of the land between 1910–15, which show the use and value of land and buildings. The assessment, called a hereditament, was entered in a Valuation Book (known as the Lloyd George 'Domesday' books). All landowners had to fill in a form, and there was a fine of £50 for not returning it.

*What information they contain*

There are two parts to the records: record maps and field books.

The record maps are based on Ordnance Survey maps – the largest scale and most recent edition available; the most common scale used was the 25-inch maps, although larger scales were used for towns. Two sets of maps are used:

◆ Working plans – these were used during the survey and contain notes about rights of way and ownership of property. The hereditament number was marked in red ink and the boundaries have a colour wash, usually red or green. The boundaries of income tax parishes are marked in yellow

- Record sheet plans – these were marked up with the boundaries and reference numbers of the hereditaments and were kept in district valuation offices.

You will need to check the map first to get the hereditament number – without that you are working pretty much in the dark. To get the map reference, you'll need to check on a map grid (available at the record office) to see which series of maps are concerned (e.g. part of Norfolk is covered by map reference 85 – shown in Roman numerals so it's LXXXV), then which of the sixteen smaller rectangles within that map reference covers the area you want (counting from left to right, row by row – e.g. Attleborough town centre is section 11).

The field book records the hereditaments; the amount of details vary between books but could include:

- Full street address
- Interior and exterior description: number and use of rooms, state of repair, date it was built and materials used, whether it has electricity or running water, and possibly a detailed plan of the building; may also describe gardens, outbuildings, outdoor sanitary arrangements (known as ECs or earth closets) and chicken runs. Industrial properties (mills, factories, shops and offices), schools and stations may be described in great detail, including cellars, fire escapes and storage areas
- Name of owner
- Name of occupier
- Date of previous sales
- Valuation figures
- Schedule of neighbouring lands owned
- Rents, who paid rates, taxes and insurance, who was liable for repairs.

At the end of a parish, public buildings and common land (such as parks and historic sites) are grouped together. The level of detail varies;

the earlier assessments are much more detailed than the later ones, basically because the project fell behind schedule and then corners were cut to bring it in on time.

The Valuation Books (known as 'Domesday Books') were the first records of the hereditaments, made from the field books; they don't contain the descriptions or plans of land and property, but can be useful in finding the hereditament number when the map hasn't survived. They are listed in parish order within income tax parishes.

*Where to find them*
- Working plans – county record offices
- Record sheet plans – National Archives. They are split by region (i.e. London is IR121, South East is IR124, Wessex is IR125, Central is IR126, Anglia is IR127, Western is IR128, West Midland is IR129, East Midland is IR130, Welsh is IR131, Liverpool is IR132, Manchester is IR133, Yorkshire is IR134 and Northern is IR135). Within each region there are up to 22 districts
- Field books – National Archives, series IR58
- Valuation books – county record offices.

*Potential difficulties*
Surveys carried out in the earlier part of the valuation exercise are more detailed than later ones, because by 1912 the valuation was running well behind schedule. Records don't exist for all areas – some were destroyed during the Second World War.

## Using town plans
These were produced from late 1500s and show the layout of the streets, including street names. Many more were produced in the 19th century as towns expanded. They were paid for by subscription.

*What information they contain*
Street names, plus local public buildings such as churches, workhouses, almshouses and hospitals, town halls, castles, gaols and lunatic asylum. They may show the buildings in great detail; they may also list subscribers' names.

*Where to find them*
Some in county record offices; there are also collections in the London Metropolitan Archives and the British Library.

*Potential difficulties*
Some show proposed redevelopments which might not have taken place.

## Using Ogilby road maps

In the 16th and 17th century, small-scale maps were produced by the likes of John Speed and Christopher Saxton. In 1675, John Ogilby produced 'An Illustration of the Kingdom of England and Dominion of Wales: by a Geographical and Historical Description of the Principal Roads thereof' (sometimes called 'Britannia'), which consisted of 1-inch strip maps. A strip map is simply a diagram of how to go from one destination to another – your route and destination are already chosen for you (whereas with modern maps, you look at your start point and your destination ad make your own choice about which route to take). There are over 100 maps in the series, showing the routes between principal places in England and Wales.

*What information they contain*
Information about the roads, including:

◆ Cross roads and road intersections
◆ Mileposts

- Villages and towns though which the roads pass
- Hills
- Mountains and forests
- Rivers, streams, and fords
- Bridges – including type, e.g. stone arches, wooden with rails.

*Where to find them*

Some may be online (e.g. Lancashire has an example at http://libweb.lancs.ac.uk/maps/ogilby1.jpg); you may also be able to buy them from one of the archive CD specialist firms.

## Using Goad maps

From 1965 the Department for Trade and Industry commissioned plans of shopping centres in the UK from Goad & Co. They were based on the Ordnance Survey maps but also included greater details – such as the use to which commercial premises were put, and the materials from which buildings were constructed.

*What information they contain*

The layout of the town centre plus details of the occupiers and business. They are updated every one or two years.

*Where to find them*

They can be found in local record offices.

*Potential difficulties*

They may be subject to the surveyor's views of an occupier's trade; they also don't take into account multiple occupation of a site (e.g. each storey of a three-story building may be different businesses).

### Using street directories

Town plans survive in some street directories (though in many library copies the map has been torn out). See Chapter 8.

## LOOKING AT OTHER SOURCES OF MAPS AND PLANS (PRIVATE ESTATE MAPS, ROAD ORDER MAPS)

### Using deposited plans

From 1792, if you wanted to build a canal, turnpike, railway or dock, you had to deposit plans with the clerk of peace as part of your building application.

### Using road order maps

These were made when orders were made to close or divert roads and footpaths, often as part of an enclosure scheme

### Using private estate maps

Between the end of the 16th century and the middle of the 19th century, estates produced maps of the property with a 'terrier' (or book) listing tenants and holdings.

### Looking at the information maps and plans contain

- Deposited plans: strip maps with a book of reference giving details of parcels of land (acreage, owner, occupier, usage)
- Road order maps: show the land affected and sometimes include the names of owners and occupiers; they may come with a schedule giving a very detailed description of each road and path in the area
- Private estate maps – details of tenants, holdings, and sometimes mention the owners of adjoining properties; may describe acreage and land, property on the land (such as barns and cottages), woods, roads, paths and water; may also have rent rolls (schedules listing tenants, rents paid/due, description of land and buildings); maps may contain drawings such as churches and manor houses.

## Finding them

They can be found at local record offices. Some local governments (such as Norfolk) also have online sites so you can view and compare different maps, including Series One Ordnance Survey maps, tithe maps and enclosure maps.

## Avoiding the potential difficulties

◆ Deposited plans – railways plans are very detailed, but often the plans submitted by railways were never built

◆ Road order maps – tend to survive from the 18th century onwards – anything earlier may not survive

◆ Private estate maps – don't survive for all parishes; plus if not deposited at the local record office, they may still be in private hands.

# Looking at Street Directories

This chapter covers the use of street directories – what they contain, how to find them, and tips for working with them.

## UNDERSTANDING THE GROWTH OF DIRECTORIES

Directories started being published in the 18th century as towns grew and there was a need for information about local trade and industries. The first provincial directory was James Sketchley's Birmingham survey in 1763, but most started from around the 1780s. The first London directory was published in 1677; however directories tended to be updated sporadically and very few guides were published annually until about the 1830s.

The earlier register offices kept lists of tradespeople, and some directories grew out of these lists; other directories were published by entrepreneurs who spotted a gap in the market and filled the need. Some directory publishers added to already published lists by going round the town and noting the tradespeople and their addresses; others asked tradespeople to send in their details with a small payment if they wanted to be included in the directories.

## LOOKING AT VARIOUS TYPES OF DIRECTORIES

There are several different types of directories:

◆ Commercial directories – these list merchants and traders

- Professional directories – these list mainly the gentry, weathy trades-people and professionals, and may list addresses but not occupations
- General trade directories – these list both 'private residents' and trades
- Specialist directories – these list tradespeople in specific industries
- Town directories – these list information only for one town or city rather than a county or part of a county (for example, *The Norwich Directory or Gentlemen and Tradesmen's Assistant*, printed by William Chase in March 1783)
- National and provincial directories – these covered several towns within a region, or perhaps a county.

The major series of directories covering the country are those produced by Frederick Kelly. Kelly initially started his directories through his work at the Post Office – he was the chief inspector of letter carriers, based in London. Letter carriers delivered his forms during postal rounds, and delivered the finished directories; he stopped using post office workers in 1847, but by then he was the dominant directory supplier for the south.

James Pigot's directories had a wide coverage in the north of the country from 1820 to the mid-1800s, and his directories tend to be a classified list of trades, with an index of names for larger towns only. His directories were produced every six or seven years after a new survey; his firm was taken over by Kelly's in 1853 (although Pigot's name was kept until 1882).

Other publishers (which cover smaller geographical areas – often as *Commercial Directory of [Town/County]*) include:

- Bailey
- Bennett
- Cowell
- Deacon
- Freebody
- Gillman
- Glover
- Gore
- Harrod & Co
- Hunt & Co
- Jakeman & Carver
- Lascelles
- Littlebury
- Lucy
- Mathews

- Melville & Co
- Owen
- Peck
- Robson
- Rusher
- Slater
- Spencers
- Spennell
- Ward
- Warren
- Webster & Co
- Whellan
- White
- Wright.

## LOOKING AT THE INFORMATION THE DIRECTORIES CONTAIN

*White's 1845 Norfolk* is a good example of one of the larger directories. Its contents are typical of a large directory and include:

- A table showing the distances of market towns within the county, from each other and from London; the market days are also noted
- Index of places – alphabetical list of the parishes, towns, townships, villages, hamlets, manors, seats, hundreds and unions in the county
- Index of subjects – including buildings, institutions, famous people, events
- Index to the history of larger towns
- General information about the county as whole ('General History and Description of the County'), which includes:
  - Statistical information
    1. Hundreds, in alphabetical order: number of, assessable acres, gross estimated rental, assessed rental, assessed to property and income tax, population

2. Unions (i.e. from Poor Law), in alphabetical order: number of parishes, population, number of houses, annual expenditure, potential room in workhouses, number of inmates in workhouses

3. General statistical information – population, births, deaths, houses, marriages, paupers, poor rate levied and spent, county rates and major expenditure (e.g. alterations and repairs to prisons and hospitals, cost of officers)

– Geography – physical situation, rivers, soils
– Parliamentary – divisions, polling places within the divisions, number of MPs returned
– General history from pre-Roman times, including the Norman Conquest
– Earls and dukes of the county
– Buildings and ancient monuments – encampments, Roman roads and stations, castles
– Historical events (brief summary – dealt with in more depth under the major towns)
– Ecclesiastic information – for example number of livings, number of nonconformist churches
– Climate and aspect
– Minerals and fossils
– Coast and rivers
– Railways
– Turnpikes
– Agriculture and enclosures (including crops, produce and fish)
– Manufacturers
– Members of Parliament and their town residences
– Magistrates and public officers
– Peers and their seats
– Seats of the nobility, gentry and clergy (listed in place order)
◆ History of the capital of the county, including:
  – Geography – physical situation, rivers, soils

- Buildings and churches
- Parliamentary wards and parishes within them
- Population statistics for the previous 150 years for the parishes
- Origins of the city
- Events in history (including plague, fire, flood, riots)
- Manufacturing in the city
- Transport links (rivers, rail)
- Municipal government
- Important buildings (particularly if something had been rebuilt)
- Ecclesiastical history – former monastic settlements, descriptions of cathedral, parish churches and nonconformist chapels, list of bishops and their dates
- Schools and hospitals/infirmaries (including lying-in hospitals and asylums) – when they were established, how they were set up and funded
- Charities and bequests – who gave the money, when, who the trustees are, and the use of the money
- Banks and financial institutions – when they were set up, where they're established, presidents of provident institutions
- Workhouses – including statistics about number of inmates and financial transactions
- Recent changes in roads
- Literary institutions (e.g. libraries, book societies – when and where they were established, how many volumes, subscription fees
- Newspapers
- Entertainment ('places of amusement') – theatres, gardens, races, regattas
- Short biographies of leading citizens
- List of streets (in alphabetical order)
- Directory of gentry, clergy, partners in firms (after the first world war, this section tends to be known as 'Private Residents')

- Classification of trades and professions (in alphabetical order from Academies to Yeast makers; within that, alphabetical order of surnames and brief address; note that pubs and inns are often listed separately)
- Lists of coaches, railway, steam packets, trading vessels and carriers
- List of local governors – mayor, aldermen, wards and councillors, Justices of the Peace
- Index of persons from the trades directory (so you can find someone by name without having to guess at their trade)
- Advertisements (which may also give you information about shop fronts and the size of a factory).

There are similar sections for other large towns in the county, and then for the parishes within each hundred, giving parochial histories and other information such as:

- Situation, extent and population of the boroughs, towns and villages
- Owners of land and lords of the manors
- Churches, chapels, charities and public institutions.

Following the history of each parish, there is a small directory giving addresses and occupations of principal inhabitants; post office regulations; arrival and departure of coaches, carriers, steam packets and trading vessels.

From the end of the 19th century, the directories started to add street directories – roads arranged in alphabetical order, with each house listed together with either the householder or a business name – followed by a classified directory of trades within the county.

Some directories also include maps, which can be useful for comparison with other forms of maps to see how streets and buildings changed.

## FINDING DIRECTORIES

The main sources of directories are:

◆ Libraries (local studies centres)
◆ Record offices (often not such a detailed collection as those in local studies centres)
◆ CD suppliers
◆ Internet – particularly the University of Leicester access project at www.historicaldirectories.org

If you want your own copies of directories, you may be able to find them at second-hand and antiquarian booksellers. Originals – particularly from earlier years – can be expensive and their condition can be variable. Some companies produced facsimiles and reprints (for example, David and Charles reprinted *White's 1845 Norfolk* in 1969), and these facsimiles can be found via second-hand and antiquarian booksellers.

## WORKING WITH DIRECTORIES

Directory listings can help you trace the movements of a particular family, or the change in occupiers in a particular address. They're useful for confirming an address from a census return, or giving additional details about a business. And the general history at the beginning of the book can be useful as a starting point (or confirmation) to glean details of people or events in a town's history.

The two basic historical techniques for directories are:

◆ Longitudinal analysis – tracing a person, business or street changes over a period of time by comparing entries between directories
◆ Cross-sectional analysis – taking a snapshot of what's happening in an area at a particular time and comparing it with a similar snapshot at a later time.

The two different types of data you can glean from directories are:

◆ Quantitative – something that can be measured or categorised, such as the number of shops in a street or the number of people listed under a particular occupation
◆ Qualitative – using information from directories to support a line of argument.

However, there are a few problems you need to be aware of:

◆ There are often gaps in a series of directories available at a library
◆ Earlier directories aren't as detailed as later ones – for example, they might list a tradesperson but wouldn't list a labourer or servant
◆ Not all directories are representative of the social or economic structure of a town or parish: it's hard to evaluate how accurate and reliable they are (although larger firms such as Kelly's used professional agents so they're likely to be more consistent and accurate than one-off directories produced by a single firm)
◆ The suburbs tend to be less well covered than town centres
◆ Directories were prepared up to a year before publication, so the information might be out of date; other directories simply reprinted lists that were out of date
◆ Details aren't always reliable – street numbering in particular can be a problem as it's either unreliable or missing
◆ There are fewer directories available after the Second World War, mainly due to the rise of free Post Office (and, later, telephone) directories
◆ Individuals can be double-counted if their business involved more than one trade – for example, agricultural machine makers and iron/brass founders; coachmakers who also kept a hotel or inn; or a bricklayer who was also a shopkeeper
◆ Sometimes people are included under the alphabetical trades listing but are missing from the street listing

- Occupation categories change – particularly in the weaving industry, where businesses might be listed one year as a manufacturer, but later as a crape manufacturer, camlet manufacturer or silk manufacturer
- Later directories put the entries of larger businesses in bold type, but it's hard to judge the scale of a business; plus entries in bold were often connected to entries which had advertisements.

## Putting it all together

Tracing a business is best done backwards. For example, Bacon's House at 31 Colegate, Norwich, is on the corner of Calvert Street, opposite St George's Church Colegate. I know from a secondary source that it's been leased to the City Club since the restoration of the building in 1978. What about before then? A trawl through the directories showed:

- *Kelly's Directory* 1971/2 – number 31 isn't mentioned, though Mrs R Meek, newsagent, is listed at number 29.
- *Kelly's Directory* 1968 – as 1971/2
- *Kelly's Directory* 1960 – as 1971/2 (though number 29 is Mrs R Beaumont, newsagent).
- *Kelly's Directory* 1950 – 31 is Sydney Starling, boot manufacturer
- *Kelly's Directory* 1939 – 31 is Sydney Starling and also Scopes & Son, leather manufacturer
- *Kelly's Directory* 1937 – 31 is Scopes & Son
- *Kelly's Directory* 1929 – 31 is Thomas Daynes, antique dealer
- *Kelly's Directory* 1927 – 31 is Thomas Daynes, boot and shoe manufacturer, and also Baxter's Leather Co Ltd, leather merchants
- *Kelly's Directory* 1922 – as 1927
- Kelly's Directory 1916 – 31 is Baxter's Leather Co Ltd and also the Linen Thread Company Ltd
- *Kelly's Directory* 1908 – 31 is Gibbs and Waller printers
- *Kelly's Directory* 1900 – 31 isn't mentioned (though 29 is Henry Ebenezer Hunt, gas fitter)

◆ *Kelly's Directory* 1896 – the street list shows Frederick Robert Segger, boot manufacturer, at number 31

Further back it becomes harder to trace who owned it. In *White's Directory* of 1890 and *Kelly's Directory* of 1892 there's a listing for wholesale and export boot and shoe manufacturer Howlett & White – but *Kelly's Directory* of 1900 lists them at number 48, so it's unlikely to be them.

*White's Directory* of 1883 lists William Warren Freeston, boot and shoe manufacturers, in Colegate; but in *White's Directory* of 1890 and *Kelly's Directory* of 1892 he's listed at 17 Colegate so he's unlikely to be the occupier of number 31.

*White's Directory* of 1883 also lists Stephen Armes, boot, shoe & upper manufacturer, in Colegate Street; but in *White's Directory* of 1890 he's listed at 28 (and in *Kelly's Directory* of 1892, number 28 is listed as Henry Houghton, boot & shoe manufacturers).

Another listed manufacturer in *White's Directory* of 1883 is Thomas Rowland Ford, boot and shoe manufacturers; he's not mentioned by 1890, but *Harrod's Directory* of 1877 refers to a Wm F. Ford & Son, so it's possible that Thomas is the 'son' from there. There's no street number listing, so this would have to be listed as a 'possible', to be followed up by using a different set of records – such as newspaper advertisements, title deeds and census information.

# ⑨

# Looking at Local
# Newspaper Archives

This chapter covers the use of local newspaper archives – sources, what to expect from the newspapers, and practical tips for working with them.

## UNDERSTANDING WHAT TO EXPECT FROM LOCAL NEWSPAPERS

The oldest provincial newspapers date from the early 18th century (the *Norwich Post*, widely regarded as the first provincial newspaper, was first published in 1701) and they consist of a single folded sheet, usually produced on a Saturday, with two columns per page. They contain a mixture of local, national and international news (the latter two reprinted from London papers) and can be very rich in local detail. For example, the *Norwich Mercury* for Saturday 13 December 1738 has two pages of international (foreign affairs) and London news. On the third page, the first half of column one is London news; then there's a local list of births this week (split between male and female), and burials (split by 10-year groupings, i.e. those under 10, aged 10–20, 20–30 etc.) and a total split by male and female. The rest of pages two and three are advertisements – which include Mr Ellis the coroner announcing that he's moved but will continue his 'surgery and Apothecary's business', advertisements for theatrical productions, and advertisements for new pubs or entertainments, and farms and businesses to let (with details of the property and stock). Some of the theatrical acts have enormously detailed descriptions. Most of page 4 contains advertisements, including sale of liquor and a note of rents; many of the ads relate to the printing and pharmaceutical business of the newspaper owner – for example *The Oxford Almanack*, Dr Bateman's Pectoral Drops (for colds), Angelical Tincture (for coughs), and a list by the publisher of what he can print.

By 1800, newspapers had grown in sheet size and fonts had decreased in size – so although the *Norwich Mercury* for Saturday 4 January 1800 is still only four pages long, there are five narrow columns per page and a lot more information crammed in. Again, it's a mixture of local and national news; page one contains advertisements (including one for the English State Lottery), and notifications of state business (such as Great Ellingham Inclosure). On page 2, the first column contains assize figures for bread and corn, a bill of mortality for the week and – as it's the first newspaper of the year – figures for the previous year. There is also information about London prices and the stock exchange. The second half of the fifth column deals with schools, and the remainder of the page deals with London news. Page 3 gives information about quarter sessions and local news – including ships and cargoes into the port of Wells, people who had to go to hospital and why (such as Thomas Gill, who had a compound fractured leg because a loaded wagon of coal ran him over), and a note of people fined for selling light measures of bread. The second half of column three contains news from other local places (such as Yarmouth and Cambridge); the first half of column four is 'letters to the editor', and the remainder of the page includes notices such as those of subscription balls, assemblies and land tax collections. Page 4 is entirely London news.

## Understanding stamp duty and changes in circulation

Stamp duty had a big effect on the circulation of local newspapers. The first tax started in 1712, at just $\frac{1}{2}$d a copy; it was increased in 1797 to $3\frac{1}{2}$d and again in 1815 to 4d a copy, which meant that newspapers cost 6d or 7d, so only the rich could afford to buy them. William Cobbet began publishing his weekly *Political Register* in 1816 for 2d a copy, and John and Leigh Hunt, publishers of the *Examiner*, called attention on their front page to what they called 'a tax on knowledge'.

More and more publishers evaded the stamp duty, and in 1819 Parliament passed the Six Acts to try to reduce the circulation of radical newspapers and pamphlets. The publishers had to deposit a bond with the government as surety against conviction for sedition or libel – £300 for London publishers and £200 for provincial publishers. The stamp duty was stated as 4d on all journals sold for less than 6d, appeared more frequently than every 26 days, or contained 'any Public News, Intelligence or Occurrences, or any Remarks or Observations thereon, or upon any Matter in Church or State'.

Selling an unstamped journal meant a fine of £20, but only the Attorney-General or Stamp Office official could start a prosecution – so a blind eye was often turned to pro-Government publications evading the duty whereas radical publishers ended up in prison. There were also taxes on advertisements and the paper itself, so the cost of newspapers limited their circulation.

Campaigns were mounted against the duty, which was reduced to 1d on newsapapers (and removed for journals) in 1836; this led to a huge increase in the number of newspapers. The duty was finally abolished in 1855, and then the number of newspapers grew rapidly; by 1870 most villages had at least a 'share' in a regional paper.

The number of newspapers decreased after around the 1950s when the cost of producing the newspapers tended to be greater than the income from advertisements and sales.

## Looking at the contents of newspapers

Local newspapers are very rich pickings for the local historian – there is often a wealth of detail about people, places and events. You can see the changes in trade through different advertisements, and social changes through the announcements and leisure activities. The 19th-century newspapers are particularly good for studies of crime and politics, because speeches and trials are reported verbatim.

The kind of things you will find in the local newspapers include:

◆ Court and government announcements
◆ Grants of peerages
◆ Obituaries (these don't always have to be local worthies; for example, in January 1874 the *Norfolk Chronicle* reported the death of Susannah Stevenson of Neale's Square, who died at the age of 105: 'a few days ago she repeated no less than 30 verses which she had learned at school 95 years ago'.)
◆ Notices of weddings
◆ Births and deaths
◆ Notable events – fires, epidemics, accidents, railways (and these might shed more light on what was happening in the city in the time: for example, in May 1852, the *Norfolk Chronicle* reported a fire at the Norfolk Hotel in St Giles' Street, and added that 'the Watch Committee held an inquiry into allegations of a deficiency in the water supply and inefficiency of the engines')
◆ Criminal trials (usually reported verbatim – general sessions and assizes. The execution was usually covered as well, and the *Norfolk Chronicle* protested about the spectators of William Thompson's execution in April 1854: 'more scenes of drunkenness and immorality were exhibited than had been seen for a long time previously in Norwich')
◆ Lists of people killed in wars or awarded medals

- Notices of bankruptcies
- Advertisements for local activities (e.g. events, clubs, societies) and local trades
- Sales of farms or businesses
- Information about licensing (e.g. if a pub received or was refused a licence – and why: for example, the *Norfolk Chronicle* in 1908 reported that the Bear and Staff pub lost its licence because it was used by 'women of ill repute' and convicted criminals)
- Enclosure (or 'inclosure') notices
- Information about collection of tax assessments
- Information about public buildings (for example, the *Norfolk Chronicle* reported in 1857 that the first sod was turned by Mr A. A. H. Beckwith – the governor of Norwich Court of Guardians – for the main front of the new Norwich Workhouse; and in June 1861 they reported a discovery at St Gregory's Church during restorations; the organ was removed so workers could clean the wall, and they found wall paintings from the 15th century showing a fight between St George and the Dragon. The reporter's verdict was that 'the figures are life-size and the colours and drawing exceedingly good'.)

## WORKING WITH NEWSPAPERS

Previous copies of local newspapers are available on microfilm nowadays to preserve the originals. The print tends to be in a very small font (particularly for the mid- to late 19th century) and can be very wearing to read for long periods. Very few local newspapers are digitised and searchable – though it might be worth doing a broad-brush search in *The Times* to see if an event made national news, in which case you can pin the date down in the local newspaper to the period between the week prior to the report in *The Times* and the week after.

Some local newspapers have been indexed by students or library staff as part of research projects so, if you are looking at a particular person or a particular type of event, you may be able to locate the information quickly through an index rather than having to search through reels and reels of film.

Antiquarians occasionally produce 'annals' – a kind of digest of newspapers, which can help you to pinpoint the date of the event and then look up more detailed information in the microfilm copy of the newspaper. (See Chapter 5, page 111, for more details.)

## Avoiding the potential difficulties

It is possible to print copies from microfilm, but it tends to be very expensive – you need to magnify the pages in order for the photocopy to be legible, so you may end up with 12 A4 sheets covering just one page of newspaper print. A large trial (such as that of James Blomfield Rush in Norwich following the murder in 1848) could run across several pages.

Your local archive may not have every edition in a series of newspapers and some older newspapers may be damaged; if the original owner of the newspaper had ticked off things while reading through or circled bits of interest, some words may be illegible.

Obituaries aren't always reliable, because often the information was provided to the newspaper by family and friends – who clearly wanted to paint a rosy picture of the deceased's life.

If quoting from a newspaper, remember the laws of copyright:

- For an unsigned (anonymous author) article: copyright expires 70 years from the end of the calendar year in which the work was made, or made available to the public. So a newspaper published in 1920 was out of copyright in 1991.
- For a signed article: copyright expires 70 years from the end of the calendar year in which the author died.

The main problem here is ownership. If the journalist was a staff reporter, the copyright probably belongs to the publisher. If the journalist was a freelancer, it probably still belongs to the author. If the article was commissioned, it is more complex – you need to take advice from library staff.

## FINDING SOURCES OF LOCAL NEWSPAPERS

- Local library/records office
- Online at the British Library website (though availability is limited)
- The British Library's Newspaper Library at Colindale
- Some intranet archives (containing abstracts or full articles) of more recent issues may be available at local library computer terminals – be aware that these articles are likely to be in copyright
- Some local newspapers may be available online – for example the Newspaper Detectives have various 19th-century editions of the *Surrey Advertiser* at http://www.newspaperdetectives.co.uk

10

# Looking at Oral History

This chapter covers the use of oral history – what it is, how to prepare for an interview, equipment, setting up the interview, doing the interview, copyright issues, working with the information and where to get more help.

## LOOKING AT WHAT ORAL HISTORY IS

According to the Oral History Society, oral history is people's memories – the kind of history we gather as we go through life. It's important because it includes the everyday events which are often ignored in textbooks, and also includes people who might have been ignored on grounds of race, disability and unemployment.

## PREPARING TO RESEARCH

When you are planning a project, the local radio or newspaper can put you in touch with people who remember the event or might have material; curators and library staff may also be able to suggest sources.

Read around your subject and make a list of questions you want to ask to get more information, but don't be too rigid about it – as the interview develops you may find more information coming out. But do keep the interview going along a loose structure, otherwise you might not get answers to the questions you wanted to ask.

## CHOOSING INTERVIEW EQUIPMENT

Use an audio recorder if you can. For a start, you won't be able to write as fast as your subject speaks (or be able to read your notes easily afterwards); using an audio recorder also helps you with eye contact and positive body language that might help encourage your subject. It is possible to use video, but your subject may be camera-shy! If you don't have your own equipment, you may be able to borrow something from your local oral history group or sound archive.

Use an external microphone. If you're holding a one-to-one interview indoors, use a lapel microphone; if the interview takes place outside, use a unidirectional hand-held microphone as it will pick up less noise.

Take advice from your local oral history group about which recording equipment to use. Tapes are being phased out; Digital Audio Tape (DAT) is already obsolete; minidisc is good but you'll need to transfer it to a CD-ROM or another medium that's likely to last. The Oral History Society recommends using gold rather than silver CD-ROMs.

## SETTING UP THE INTERVIEW

Initial contact by phone is best. Say who you are, what your project is, the kind of things you'd like to talk about. It is best to say you want a chat about the past or the story of their life – the word 'interview' can put people off.

Agree when and where you will do the interview. It's best to make it somewhere the interviewee is comfortable. Keep the interview one-to-one – unless the subject is a child, in which case the parent or guardian should also be present.

The Oral History Society advise that it's unethical (and sometimes illegal) to use interviews without the informed consent of the person you're interviewing – so your interviewee needs to know exactly what you're planning to do with the information (e.g. giving a copy to the local sound archive, or publishing part or all of the interview in print, in broadcast or on the internet). It's a good idea to use a clearance form (see page 156 below).

## WORKING BEFORE THE INTERVIEW

Reassure your subject, who might be feeling very apprehensive – particularly if it's a first interview. Pick a quiet place where there's no TV or audio on, and away from street noise if possible. Sit side by side; and, if using hand-held microphone, make sure it's not on a hard surface or it may affect the recording.

## DOING THE INTERVIEW

- Keep questions short and clear
- Use open questions (i.e. which can't be answered with yes or no)
- Don't interrupt – wait for a pause before asking the next question
- Use positive body language – nods and smiles
- Don't rush
- Don't contradict or get into an argument with your subject
- Be sensitive and respect confidences
- Try to make smooth transitions between subjects.

## THE INTERVIEW ITSELF

- Use a chronological structure
- Check your subject's age, date of birth, place of birth, what their parents' jobs were, and what their own main jobs were
- Get people to tell you about their personal experiences (eyewitness testimony) rather than things they may have heard from someone else
- Don't ask leading questions or make leading statements, for example, 'You were poor so you must have had a miserable childhood.' Instead ask 'Tell me about your childhood'
- If you want to know about a person's life, you need to structure the interview and you may need several sessions, such as

- Begin with their early life (family background, brothers and sisters, parents, grandparents, aunts and uncles, cousins)
- Home (where they lived, what the house was like, what they ate)
- Leisure (games, friends, weekends, holidays, special occasions)
- School (where, teachers, friends, favourite subjects)
- Religion (church, Sunday school)
- Working life (first job, what sort of things they did at work)
- Family life (marriage, children, home etc.)

- Ask questions to get the facts (e.g. 'Where did you live?')
- Ask questions to get comments and opinions (e.g. 'Can you describe the house?' 'What was he like as a person?' 'Why did you move?' 'How did you feel?')

## WORKING AFTER THE INTERVIEW

- Thank your subject but don't rush away
- Give them your contact phone number and address
- Say if you're coming back for a further interview or not
- Tell them how the interview is going to be preserved (e.g. a copy deposited in the local sound archives and copy kept on your computer), and what you're going to do with the interview (use for research, publish or broadcast it, transcribe it)
- Write down any restrictions the interviewee asks for (e.g. no publication on the internet)
- Talk about copyright and clearance – it's a good idea to get a clearance form signed, i.e. stating that you can use the recordings
- Give a copy or transcript to the interviewee if they ask for one.

## WORKING WITH FILES

- Back up your files – especially if using digital files (such as flash-card recorders) – on a computer system as well as on a CD-ROM or DVD-ROM

♦ Label your files – subject's full name and date of birth, place and date of interview, your name, type of equipment used

♦ Write a synopsis of the interview – list in order the main themes, topics and stories discussed; make sure this is labelled so you can match it to the audio file afterwards.

## LOOKING AT COPYRIGHT AND LEGAL ASPECTS

There are separate copyrights for the words spoken and for the actual recording. The person who owns the words spoken is the speaker; the person who owns the recording is the person or organisation who arranged for it to be made. Copyright of transcriptions belong to the owner of the words spoken.

Copyright lasts for 70 years after the end of the year in which the speaker died; if the material was recorded before 1 August 1989, copyright lasts until 50 years from the end of 1989 or 70 years after the death of the speaker, whichever is the longest. So you need to be sure that your interviewee agrees that you can use their words, make copies of the recordings and publish the material (either in written form, broadcast form, exhibition or through the internet).

Under the Copyright Act 1988 you also need to make sure you don't edit, adapt or alter the material to give any false impressions – regardless of who owns the copyright.

Under the Data Protection Act 1998 you need to get permission before publishing the interview if your subject (or anyone else they're talking about) can be identified as individuals.

Be aware of the problems of defamation. If in any doubt, take advice from your local sound archive, local history group or an organisation such as the Society of Authors.

## Clearance form

A good format to use would be:

---

[Interviewer name/project name] is grateful for your contribution of an oral history recording. As you know the recording/transcript will be preserved for posterity and used in the project.

Under the 1988 Copyright Act [I/we] need to seek your written permission to use the recording. This does not restrict any use you may wish to make of the information you gave [me/us], but it lets [me/us] ensure your contribution is preserved for posterity and used in the project and in accordance with your wishes.

[Description of items, e.g. 'John Smith's recollection of High Street, Anytown, 1953–60']

Do you have any objection to your contribution being used for:

| | |
|---|---|
| A resource for research purposes | Yes/No |
| Educational use in schools, colleges etc | Yes/No |
| Reference and as a source of information for publications | Yes/No |
| Use on [the project's] website | Yes/No |
| Do you wish to remain anonymous? | Yes/No |
| Do you wish to make any time restrictions before your contribution is released? | Yes/No |
| Would you be willing to assign your copyright to [project/archive], which will allow [project/archive] to use your recording/transcript? | Yes/No |

Signed . . . . . . . . . . . . . . . . . . . . .
Print name . . . . . . . . . . . . . . . .
Address. . . . . . . . . . . . . . . . . . . .
Postcode. . . . . . . . . . . . . . . . . . .
Telephone. . . . . . . . . . . . . . . . .

---

## WORKING WITH INFORMATION

Check dates, names and details of events against another source to verify them – people don't always remember things exactly.

People are often better at remembering faces than names. So if you're trying to trace the history of a school, for example, you might show someone a picture of their class or sports team, which might jog their memories.

## FINDING OUT WHERE TO GET MORE HELP

The Oral History Society and British Sound Library Archive hold training courses around the country every year about how to interview people. Contact the Oral History Society or your local sound archive to see if there's a course near you (see pages 117 and 170 for contact details).

# 11

# Using the Internet

This chapter covers the use of the internet and practical tips to maximise the pros and minimise the cons.

Firstly, remember that the internet is a research tool, not a research substitute, so it should only form *part* of your research. Most records are still in paper format or microform rather than digitised, so you will still have to go and look at them physically. Some records are digitised, but they may only be viewable on a subscription or pay-per-view basis.

One of the most common uses for the internet in local historian terms is to browse catalogues and indexes to help you find the paper/microform document you need to look at and where it's located. If you are checking online databases, remember that the database is only as good as the keywords typed in; and there may be variant spellings, particularly with place names and personal names.

## USING GATEWAYS

Gateways give good subject-specific access to the internet. They tend to be maintained by organisations, and the websites on the list are selected for their relevance and quality. Intute (www.intute.ac.uk/artsandhumanities) is a particularly good gateway for historians.

## USING SEARCH ENGINES

Search engines such as Google are very useful for trawling the internet to find relevant articles. However, you can spend a lot of time hunting for documents if you're not careful with your search criteria!

### Using keyword searches

You type in the words you want to search for and the search engine brings up a list of documents. For example, supposing I wanted to see what was online about Bacon's house (31 Colegate, Norwich). Searching 'the web' for 'history' brought up 1,170 million sites. Narrowing my search to just 'pages from the UK' cut the list to 119 million – still too many if I only wanted to find out about the history of Norwich. Searching for 'history + Norwich' brought the list down to 2.8 million. Making my search more specific (history + Norwich + Colegate) brought it down to 21,000 sites. Making it more specific still (history + Norwich + Colegate + Bacon) brought it down to 169 sites – manageable, but still a little unwieldy. Changing a keyword for a phrase (history + Norwich + Colegate + "Bacon's house") brought it down to 41 sites – which were much more relevant that my original 190 million sites.

The main things to remember with search engines are:

- Keep your keywords specific
- Avoid common words
- Check whether you need to put a phrase in double quote marks (so the search will match your phrase exactly)
- Consider spelling – place names and personal names in particular can vary. Truncation and word-stemming can help here (i.e. searching for words that have the same prefix or suffix, using * as the wildcard character: so Brit* would bring up words such as Britain, Britannia, British, Brittany, Brittle).

## ANALYSING A WEBSITE CRITICALLY

Be critical when you're reading material. Anyone can publish anything on the internet, so personal pages are often less reliable than those of official organisations. Some personal sites are excellent (such as the Plunketts' site about historical Norwich, which includes a lot of images and is meticulously researched – www.the-plunketts.freeserve.co.uk/); others are enthusiastic but inaccurate, so always check dates and substantiate facts. (And remember that text and images online are all subject to copyright.)

When evaluating a website, look at similar criteria to the ones you'd use for evaluating printed material:

- ◆ Authority – who hosts the page? The URL (website address) should show you who put up the page or if they're associated with an organisation. An address ending 'ac.uk' means it's a British academic institution; 'edu' is an American academic institution; 'org' is a non-profit organisation; and 'co.uk' and 'com' are commercial companies. The home page should include information about the author(s), where they are based, and if they are part of an organisation or company. You should also be able to see what's on the site – images, transcriptions, articles, indexes or data. There should also be something telling you the author's credentials (e.g. a biography or bibliography), and full citations for all data used
- ◆ Purpose:
  - – Who is the material aimed at: general readers, schoolchildren, degree students, specialists or researchers?
  - – Why was it created: to inform, share information, entertain or give opinions?
- ◆ Coverage – this depends on the resource. Journal articles will be in more depth than a brief newspaper report. Articles should give you a bibliography or links so you can follow up information
- ◆ Accuracy – are the authors acknowledged specialists in their field? If the material is full of spelling and grammatical errors, the research

might be just as flawed. The authors should tell you how they gathered the information and give you the methodology and references to original datasets, so you can check the results for accuracy.

◆ Currency – how up to date is it?
   – The home page should give you the date the site was created, and possibly the dates of the last update and next planned update
   – If there are lots of broken links, the chances are the page hasn't been maintained or updated for a long while
   – The page should give the date of original publication; for transcriptions, the page should give the dates of both the original printed source and the date the digital version was compiled.

◆ Ease of navigation
   – The page should be easy to read (strange colour schemes or unusual/hard-to-read fonts usually denotes sites that are more interested in the design than the content, so it is a pointer to double-check references in the content)
   – It should be easy to find what you want on the site (via links on the home page, a site map, a search tool or a help section)
   – There should be a logical order of links from one section to the next
   – Images should be there for a purpose other than design (e.g. to show an example of a record or map).

Be aware that not all electronic journals give free access to all articles. You may be able to search abstracts free of charge to help you decide if you need to see the full article.

## USING TRANSCRIPTIONS
If the web page includes a transcription, it should:

- Give you the full reference for the source material
- Say which edition the transcription is based on (so you can check for accuracy/reliability)
- Tell you what (if any) editing has been done
- Tell you if any emendations have been made, where and why.

# Appendix 1

# List of Useful Websites for Local history

## GENERAL ARCHIVES INFORMATION
### National Archives
www.nationalarchives.gov.uk

Includes the Historic Manuscripts Commission and former Public Record Office. Has a detailed list of archive repositories, from local record offices and libraries through to museums and specialist archives, at www.nationalarchives.gov.uk/archon/. Also has a searchable catalogue of the collections within the National Archives. Extensive and very useful information leaflets and research guides. Also has a section for children and a palaeography tutorial.

### Scottish General Register Office
www.scotlandspeople.gov
Information about Scots archival holdings.

### Access to Archives (A2A)
www.a2a.org.uk
English strand of the UK Archives Network. You can search detailed catalogues from over 340 repositories (as well as the National Archives).

### British Library

www.bl.uk

British Library website. The catalogue listings are at www.bl.uk/
catalogues/listings.html

### Guildhall library

www.cityoflondon.gov.uk/Corporation/leisure_heritage/libraries_archives
_museums_galleries/city_london_libraries/guildhall_lib.htm

Website for the Guildhall library. Has catalogue listings plus some
useful leaflets on getting started in research.

### Archives hub

www.archiveshub.ac.uk/

Good gateway to archives – searchable.

## GENERAL HISTORICAL SOURCES (INCLUDING ASSOCIATIONS)

### British History Online

www.british-history.ac.uk/

A joint site from the Institute of Historical Research and the History of
Parliament Trust; has digital resources, which you can search by county.
Particularly good for the Victoria County History. You can also browse
some Series One Ordnance Survey maps on the site.

### British Association of Local History

www.balh.co.uk/index.php

Publishes a quarterly journal, *The Local Historian*, and a quarterly
magazine, *Local History News*. The site has membership details and
good links to national organisations and local societies.

### History.uk.com

www.history.uk.com/

Site contains a variety of historical links. There are editorial features and a timeline.

**Institute of Historical Research**
http://www.history.ac.uk/
Resources for historians including articles and an open access library.

**Local History magazine**
http://www.local-history.co.uk
Website has information leaflets and good links to local history societies and courses.

**Royal Historical Society Bibliography**
http://www.rhs.ac.uk/bibl/
Searchable bibliographical guide to what has been written about British and Irish history from the Roman period to the present day. Hosted by the Institute of Historical Research. Includes links to online catalogues.

**Victoria County History**
http://www.victoriacountyhistory.ac.uk
Has advice and information for local historians on how to get started.

## SPECIFIC AREA RESEARCH
### London's Past Online
www.history.ac.uk/cmh/lpol/
Produced by the Centre for Metropolitan History in association with the Royal Historical Society Bibliography; has a searchable database of a bibliography for London.

### Centre for English Local History: University of Leicester
www.le.ac.uk/elh/
Contains links for the sites they host.

**Centre of East Anglian Studies (CEAS)**

www1.uea.ac.uk/cm/home/schools/hum/his/ceas

Good links for Norfolk and Suffolk, including the excellent University of East Anglia-based site Virtual Norfolk http://www.webarchive.org.uk/pan/12032/20051206.virtualnorfolk.uea.ac.uk/, which includes transcriptions of many documents.

**Centre for Urban History**

www.le.ac.uk/urbanhist/

Based at the University of Leicester. Good links to local resources; online catalogue.

**Manchester Centre for Regional History**

www.mcrh.mmu.ac.uk/

Organises events – useful contact if working in the North-West but not much available online at the moment. Produces the Manchester Region History Review.

## SOURCES FOR PEOPLE, CENSUS RECORDS AND FAMILY HISTORY

### Church of Jesus Christ of Latter Day Saints (aka Family History Centres)

www.familysearch.org/

Holds searchable versions of the International Genealogical Index and the 1881 census of England and Wales.

### findmypast.com

www.findmypast.com/home.jsp

Access to the registers of births, deaths and marriages in England and Wales from 1837 to the present day (on a pay-per-view basis). Also has articles and advice on getting started.

## Rootsweb

http://freebmd.rootsweb.com

Free searchable access to the index of births, deaths and marriages in the UK. Note that the complete index has not yet been transcribed.

## Ancestry.co.uk

www.ancestry.co.uk

Access to the 1871, 1891 and 1901 censuses of England and Wales, plus other records from the 1500s onwards. Subscription site; some free (limited) databases. You will need to register. Some libraries allow their subscribers free access at the libraries.

## 1901censusoline.com

www.1901censusonline.com

It is free to search the indexes although you'll pay a small fee to see the census pages and transcripts.

## Society of Friends (Quakers)

www.quaker.org.uk

Information about the Society of Friends and their record holdings in the library. Can seach online, but if you want to go in person you need a dated letter of recommendation from 'someone of good standing in your community' – such as a letter from your minister if you are a member of another church; or from your tutor or supervisor if you are a student.

## Federation of Family History Societies

www.ffhs.org.uk/

Website has a directory of family history societies across the country.

## Familia

www.familia.org.uk/

Directory of family history resources held in public libraries.

### Genuki

www.genuki.org.uk/
Virtual reference library of information relevant to the UK and Ireland. Has good information about how to get started.

### Society of Genealogists

www.sog.org.uk
Information about the Society of Genealogists and their record holdings in the library (which you can search for a fee). Also has a range of information leaflets.

### Documents Online

www.documentsonline.pro.gov.uk
Part of the National Archives website. Has searchable indexes from the 1300s to 1858. There is a fee for downloading images.

### Cyndi's List

www.cyndislist.com
Excellent genealogical resource; has some good tips for beginners at www.cyndislist.com/beginner.htm

### *Oxford Dictionary of National Biography* (ODNB)

www.oxforddnb.com

## SOURCES FOR BUILDINGS AND ARCHITECTURE
### English Heritage

www.english-heritage.org.uk
Free site with details of listed buildings and the English Monuments Record.

### Pastscape

www.pastscape.org/
Searchable database of listed buildings and information about finds in the areas.

## Bricks and Brass

www.bricksandbrass.co.uk/

Site with architectural details for 19th and 20th century houses.

# SOURCES FOR STREET DIRECTORIES

## Historical Directories

www.historicaldirectories.org

Project from the University of Leicester that gives a searchable digital library of local and trade directories for England and Wales 1750–1919. Runs of directories are not complete but there are several directories for most areas.

# SOURCES FOR IMAGES

## Heritage Image Partnership

http://www.heritage-images.com/

Searchable library of images which you can view in thumbnail.

## Images of England

www.imagesofengland.org.uk/

Part of the English Heritage website. Digital library of photographs of England's 370,000 Listed Buildings. Has optional registration (free) for advanced search facilities.

# SOURCES FOR NEWSPAPERS

## *The Times* digital archive

www.galegroup.com/Times

Searchable resource for issues of *The Times* 1785–1985. Subscription may be accessible through your local library.

# SOURCES FOR TRIALS

## Old Bailey proceedings

www.oldbaileyonline.org

Proceedings of the Central Criminal Court in London from April 1674 to October 1834 – contains 101,102 trials which are digitised and fully searchable.

### Newgate Calendar
www.exclassics.com
Online copy of the Newgate Calendar – trials up until the 19th century.

## SOURCES FOR MAPS
### Ordnance Survey maps
www.ordsvy.gov.uk

### Digital Historical Maps
www.old-maps.co.uk
Searchable by place name, address or co-ordinate (Ordnance Survey Grid reference).

## MISCELLANEOUS
### Oral History Society
www.ohs.org.uk
Good practical tips on working with oral history.

### Pub History Society
www.pubhistorysociety.co.uk/

### Measuringworth.com
www.measuringworth.com
Excellent resource for links on purchasing power.

### BBC History Trail
www.bbc.co.uk/history/trail/local_history/
Good guides for getting started.

## English Handwriting 1500–1700

www.english.cam.ac.uk/ceres/ehoc/

Online palaeography tutorial from Cambridge University – really good! (See also the one at the National Archives website.)

## Medieval Writing

www.medievalwriting.50megs.com.writing.htm

Another good palaeography site.

## Palaeography

http://paleo.anglo-norman.org

Good tutorials from Dr Diane Tillotson.

## Vision of Britain

www.visionofbritain.org.uk/index.jsp

A vision of Britain between 1801 and 2001. Including maps, statistical trends and historical descriptions written on journeys around Britain between the 12th and 19th centuries. Using census information, the site demonstrates changes across Britain through the use of maps and graphs. Produced by the Department of Geography at the University of Portsmouth.

## London Gazette online

www.gazettes-online.co.uk

Digital archive of publication listing recipients of medals, aliens granted naturalisation and changes of name by deed poll. Free to search and view the PDF files.

# Appendix 2

# List of Useful Groups and Associations

**British Association for Local History**
BALH
PO BOX 6549
Somersal Herbert
Ashbourne
DE6 5WH
Tel: 01283 585947
Website: www.balh.co.uk

**Family And Community Historical Research Association**
The Chairman
Family & Community Historical
Research Society
Fir Trees
12 Fryer Close
Chesham
Bucks
HP5 1RD
Website: www.fachrs.com/

**Federation of Family History Societies**
PO Box 2425
Coventry
West Midlands
CV5 6YX
Tel: 01455 203133
Website: http://www.ffhs.org.uk

**Genealogical Society of Utah/Church of Jesus Christ of Latter-day Saints**
Website has details of local offices.
Website: www.familysearch.org

**The Historical Assocation**
59a Kennington Park Road
London
SE11 4JH
Tel: 020 7735 3901
Website: www.history.org.uk/

**Historical Manuscripts
Commission**
The National Archives
Kew
Richmond
Surrey
TW9 4DU
Tel: 020 8876 3444
Website: www.nationalarchives.
gov.uk/archon/

**Family Records Centre (The
National Archives)**
The National Archives
Kew
Richmond
Surrey TW9 4DU
Website: www.familyrecords.gov.uk

**General Register Office
(Scotland)**
New Register House
3 West Register Street
Edinburgh
EH1 3YT
Tel: 0131 334 0380
Website: www.gro-
scotland.gov.uk

**National Archives of Scotland**
HM General Register House
2 Princes Street
Edinburgh
EH1 3YY
Tel: 0131 535 1314
Website: www.nas.gov.uk

**National Library of Wales**
Aberystwyth
Ceredigion
Wales
SY23 3BU
Tel: 01970 632800
Website: www.llgc.org.uk

**The Religious Society of Friends**
The Library
Friends House
173–177 Euston Road
London
NW1 2BJ
Tel: 020 7663 1135
Website: www.quaker.org.uk

**Society of Genealogists**
14 Charterhouse Buildings
Goswell Road
London EC1M 7BA
Tel: 020 7251 8799
Website: www/sog.org.uk

# Appendix 3

# List of Useful Reference Books

For the history of specific places, your local studies library can advise you of good sources (for example, the standard history for your county, whether a Victoria County History exists for your county, and possibly more specialised books depending on what you're looking at).

It's also worth looking at the general overview of the county's history in one of the 19th-century trade directories.

The English Place Name Society (based at the University of Nottingham) has an excellent series of books on place names for various counties, which is particularly helpful if you're looking at the derivation of street names; the bibliography in these volumes will also be useful pointers to county history.

On more general topics, the following will be useful as a starting point, or to help you interpret the various sources:

Nick Barratt, *Tracing the History of Your House*, The National Archives 2006, ISBN 1903365902.

Geraldine Beech and Rose Mitchell, *Maps for Family and Local History*, The National Archives 2004, ISBN 1900365503.

Joy Bristow, *The Local Historian's Glossary of Words and Terms*, Countryside Books 2001, ISBN 1853067075.

C. R. Cheney (revised by Michael Jones), *A Handbook of Dates for Students of British History*, Cambridge University Press reprinted 2004, ISBN 0521770955.

Mark D. Herber, *Ancestral Trails: The Complete Guide to British Genealogy and Family History*, Sutton Publishing 2005, ISBN 0750941987.

David Hey, *The Oxford Companion to Local and Family History*, Oxford University Press 2002, ISBN 0198606672.

Charles T. Martin, *The Record Interpreter*, Phillimore reprinted 1999, ISBN 0850334659.

Lionel Munby, *How Much Is That Worth?*, Phillimore 1989, ISBN 0850337410.

Pevsner, Nikolaus, *The Buildings of England series*, Penguin (various dates)

Anthony Quiney, *The Traditional Buildings of England*, Thames and Hudson 1995, ISBN 0500276617.

Philip Riden, *Record Sources for Local History*, B.T. Batsford Ltd 1987, ISBN 0713457260.

Colin Waters, *A Dictionary of Old Trades, Titles and Occupations*, Countryside Books 2002, ISBN 1853067946.

# Appendix 4

# List of Useful Dates

## DATES

Under the Calendar Act 1752, the first day of the year moved from Lady Day (25 March) to 1 January. Before then, 1 January–24 March was the last quarter of a year. So you need to add a year to convert dates in records to 'modern' times. For example, the record may show a date of 1 February 1605 (also known as 'old style'), but it's what we would know as 1 February 1606 ('new style'). It is best to write it as 1 February 1605/6 – this avoids ambiguity because then anyone reading your research will know that 1605 was written in the document but 1606 is the 'real' year in the modern calendar.

1752 was also the year when the country switched from the Julian calendar to the Gregorian calendar (see Chapter 2, page 22, for a fuller explanation).

In Scotland, 1 January was the official beginning of the year from 1600.

## REGNAL YEARS

Regnal years are often used in wills and legal documents, and in some early registers. This simply means the number of years since the coronation of the ruling monarch: and year 1 started on the day of the coronation.

From the time of Edward I in 1239, the regnal year began on the date of accession, i.e. the day the reign began, usually the day the previous monarch died. This was usually before the coronation.

Regnal years are not commonly used after about 1760, but some scholars and historians still use them.

The tables below list the regnal years from William I until the accession of Elizabeth II. Some regnal years (such as John and Charles II) have quirks, which are noted below.

## William I

25 Dec–24 Dec

| | |
|---|---|
| 1 | 1066–7 |
| 2 | 1067–8 |
| 3 | 1068–9 |
| 4 | 1069–70 |
| 5 | 1070–1 |
| 6 | 1071–2 |
| 7 | 1072–3 |
| 8 | 1073–4 |
| 9 | 1074–5 |
| 10 | 1075–6 |
| 11 | 1076–7 |
| 12 | 1077–8 |
| 13 | 1078–9 |
| 14 | 1079–80 |
| 15 | 1080–1 |
| 16 | 1081–2 |
| 17 | 1082–3 |
| 18 | 1083–4 |
| 19 | 1084–5 |
| 20 | 1085–6 |
| 21 | 1086–9 Sep 1087 |

## William II

26 Sep–25 Sep

| | |
|---|---|
| 1 | 1087–8 |
| 2 | 1088–9 |
| 3 | 1089–90 |
| 4 | 1090–1 |
| 5 | 1091–2 |
| 6 | 1092–3 |
| 7 | 1093–4 |
| 8 | 1094–5 |
| 9 | 1095–6 |
| 10 | 1096–7 |
| 11 | 1097–8 |
| 12 | 1098–9 |
| 13 | 1099–2 Aug 1100 |

## Henry I

5 Aug–4 Aug

| | |
|---|---|
| 1 | 1100–1 |
| 2 | 1101–2 |
| 3 | 1102–3 |
| 4 | 1103–4 |

| | |
|---|---|
| 5 | 1104–5 |
| 6 | 1105–6 |
| 7 | 1106–7 |
| 8 | 1107–8 |
| 9 | 1108–9 |
| 10 | 1109–10 |
| 11 | 1110–1 |
| 12 | 1111–2 |
| 13 | 1112–3 |
| 14 | 1113–4 |
| 15 | 1114–5 |
| 16 | 1115–6 |
| 17 | 1116–7 |
| 18 | 1117–8 |
| 19 | 1118–9 |
| 20 | 1119–20 |
| 21 | 1120–1 |
| 22 | 1121–2 |
| 23 | 1122–3 |
| 24 | 1123–4 |
| 25 | 1124–5 |
| 26 | 1125–6 |
| 27 | 1126–7 |
| 28 | 1127–8 |
| 29 | 1128–9 |
| 30 | 1129–30 |
| 31 | 1130–1 |
| 32 | 1131–2 |
| 33 | 1132–3 |
| 34 | 1133–4 |
| 35 | 1134–5 |
| 36 | 1135 – 1 Dec 1135 |

**Stephen**

26 Dec–25 Dec

| | |
|---|---|
| 1 | 1135–6 |
| 2 | 1136–7 |
| 3 | 1137–8 |
| 4 | 1138–9 |
| 5 | 1139–40 |
| 6 | 1140–1 |
| 7 | 1141–2 |
| 8 | 1142–3 |
| 9 | 1143–4 |
| 10 | 1144–5 |
| 11 | 1145–6 |
| 12 | 1146–7 |
| 13 | 1147–8 |
| 14 | 1148–9 |
| 15 | 1149–50 |
| 16 | 1150–1 |
| 17 | 1151–2 |
| 18 | 1152–3 |
| 19 | 1153 – 23 Oct 1154 |

**Henry II**

19 Dec–18 Dec

| | |
|---|---|
| 1 | 1154–5 |
| 2 | 1155–6 |
| 3 | 1156–7 |
| 4 | 1157–8 |
| 5 | 1158–9 |

| | |
|---|---|
| 6 | 1159–60 |
| 7 | 1160–1 |
| 8 | 1161–2 |
| 9 | 1162–3 |
| 10 | 1163–4 |
| 11 | 1164–5 |
| 12 | 1165–6 |
| 13 | 1166–7 |
| 14 | 1167–8 |
| 15 | 1168–9 |
| 16 | 1169–70 |
| 17 | 1170–1 |
| 18 | 1171–2 |
| 19 | 1172–3 |
| 20 | 1173–4 |
| 21 | 1174–5 |
| 22 | 1175–6 |
| 23 | 1176–7 |
| 24 | 1177–8 |
| 25 | 1178–9 |
| 26 | 1179–80 |
| 27 | 1180–1 |
| 28 | 1181–2 |
| 29 | 1182–3 |
| 30 | 1183–4 |
| 31 | 1184–5 |
| 32 | 1185–6 |
| 33 | 1186–7 |
| 34 | 1187–8 |
| 35 | 1188 – 6 Jul 1189 |

**Richard I**

3 Sept – 2 Sept

| | |
|---|---|
| 1 | 1189–90 |
| 2 | 1190–1 |
| 3 | 1191–2 |
| 4 | 1192–3 |
| 5 | 1193–4 |
| 6 | 1194–5 |
| 7 | 1195–6 |
| 8 | 1196–7 |
| 9 | 1197–8 |
| 10 | 1198–6 Apr 1199 |

**John**

Ascension Day – this means his regnal years are of unequal length as Ascension Day is a moveable feast. The problem here is that some years are more than a year long, so there are duplicate dates in some years and it's almost impossible to work out which date was meant.

| | |
|---|---|
| 1 | 27 May 1199–17 May 1200 |
| 2 | 18 May 1200–2 May 1201 |
| 3 | 3 May 1201–22 May 1202 |
| 4 | 23 May 1202–14 May 1203 |
| 5 | 15 May 1203–2 Jun 1204 |
| 6 | 3 Jun 1204 –18 May 1205 |

| | | | |
|---|---|---|---|
| 7 | 19 May 1205–10 May 1206 | 16 | 1231–2 |
| 8 | 11 May 1206–30 May 1207 | 17 | 1232–3 |
| 9 | 31 May 1207–14 May 1208 | 18 | 1233–4 |
| 10 | 15 May 1208–6 May 1209 | 19 | 1234–5 |
| 11 | 7 May 1209–26 May 1210 | 20 | 1235–6 |
| 12 | 27 May 1210–11 May 1211 | 21 | 1236–7 |
| 13 | 12 May 1211–2 May 1212 | 22 | 1237–8 |
| 14 | 3 May 1212–22 May 1213 | 23 | 1238–9 |
| 15 | 23 May 1213–7 May 1214 | 24 | 1239–40 |
| 16 | 8 May 1214–27 May 1215 | 25 | 1240–1 |
| 17 | 28 May 1215–18 May 1216 | 26 | 1241–2 |
| 18 | 19 May 1216–19 Oct 1216 | 27 | 1242–3 |
| | | 28 | 1243–4 |

**Henry III**

28 Oct–27 Oct

| | | | |
|---|---|---|---|
| | | 29 | 1244–5 |
| | | 30 | 1245–6 |
| | | 31 | 1246–7 |
| 1 | 1216–7 | 32 | 1247–8 |
| 2 | 1217–8 | 33 | 1248–9 |
| 3 | 1218–9 | 34 | 1249–50 |
| 4 | 1219–20 | 35 | 1250–1 |
| 5 | 1220–1 | 36 | 1251–2 |
| 6 | 1221–2 | 37 | 1252–3 |
| 7 | 1222–3 | 38 | 1253–4 |
| 8 | 1223–4 | 39 | 1254–5 |
| 9 | 1224–5 | 40 | 1255–6 |
| 10 | 1225–6 | 41 | 1256–7 |
| 11 | 1226–7 | 42 | 1257–8 |
| 12 | 1227–8 | 43 | 1258–9 |
| 13 | 1228–9 | 44 | 1259–60 |
| 14 | 1229–30 | 45 | 1260–1 |
| 15 | 1230–1 | | |

| | |
|---|---|
| 46 | 1261–2 |
| 47 | 1262–3 |
| 48 | 1263–4 |
| 49 | 1264–5 |
| 50 | 1265–6 |
| 51 | 1266–7 |
| 52 | 1267–8 |
| 53 | 1268–9 |
| 54 | 1269–70 |
| 55 | 1270–1 |
| 56 | 1271–2 |
| 57 | 1272–16 Nov 1272 |

## Edward I

20 Nov–19 Nov

| | |
|---|---|
| 1 | 1272–3 |
| 2 | 1273–4 |
| 3 | 1274–5 |
| 4 | 1275–6 |
| 5 | 1276–7 |
| 6 | 1277–8 |
| 7 | 1278–9 |
| 8 | 1279–80 |
| 9 | 1280–1 |
| 10 | 1281–2 |
| 11 | 1282–3 |
| 12 | 1283–4 |
| 13 | 1284–5 |
| 14 | 1285–6 |
| 15 | 1286–7 |
| 16 | 1287–8 |
| 17 | 1288–9 |
| 18 | 1289–90 |
| 19 | 1290–1 |
| 20 | 1291–2 |
| 21 | 1292–3 |
| 22 | 1293–4 |
| 23 | 1294–5 |
| 24 | 1295–6 |
| 25 | 1296–7 |
| 26 | 1297–8 |
| 27 | 1298–99 |
| 28 | 1299–1300 |
| 29 | 1300–1 |
| 30 | 1301–2 |
| 31 | 1302–3 |
| 32 | 1303–4 |
| 33 | 1304–5 |
| 34 | 1305–6 |
| 35 | 1306–7 Jul 1307 |

## Edward II

8 Jul–7 Jul

| | |
|---|---|
| 1 | 1307–8 |
| 2 | 1308–9 |
| 3 | 1309–10 |
| 4 | 1310–1 |
| 5 | 1311–2 |
| 6 | 1312–3 |
| 7 | 1313–4 |

| 8  | 1314–5 |
| 9  | 1315–6 |
| 10 | 1316–7 |
| 11 | 1317–8 |
| 12 | 1318–9 |
| 13 | 1319–20 |
| 14 | 1320–1 |
| 15 | 1321–2 |
| 16 | 1322–3 |
| 17 | 1323–4 |
| 18 | 1324–5 |
| 19 | 1325–6 |
| 20 | 1326–20 Jan 1327 |

**Edward III**

25 Jan–24 Jan

| 1  | 1327–8 |
| 2  | 1328–9 |
| 3  | 1329–30 |
| 4  | 1330–1 |
| 5  | 1331–2 |
| 6  | 1332–3 |
| 7  | 1333–4 |
| 8  | 1334–5 |
| 9  | 1335–6 |
| 10 | 1336–7 |
| 11 | 1337–8 |
| 12 | 1338–9 |
| 13 | 1339–40 |
| 14 | 1340–1 |
| 15 | 1341–2 |

| 16 | 1342–3 |
| 17 | 1343–4 |
| 18 | 1344–5 |
| 19 | 1345–6 |
| 20 | 1346–7 |
| 21 | 1347–8 |
| 22 | 1348–9 |
| 23 | 1349–50 |
| 24 | 1350–1 |
| 25 | 1351–2 |
| 26 | 1352–3 |
| 27 | 1353–4 |
| 28 | 1354–5 |
| 29 | 1355–6 |
| 30 | 1356–7 |
| 31 | 1357–8 |
| 32 | 1358–9 |
| 33 | 1359–60 |
| 34 | 1360–1 |
| 35 | 1361–2 |
| 36 | 1362–3 |
| 37 | 1363–4 |
| 38 | 1364–5 |
| 39 | 1365–6 |
| 40 | 1366–7 |
| 41 | 1367–8 |
| 42 | 1368–9 |
| 43 | 1369–70 |
| 44 | 1370–1 |
| 45 | 1371–2 |
| 46 | 1372–3 |
| 47 | 1373–4 |

48  1374–5
49  1375–6
50  1376–7
51  1377–21 Jun 1377

**Richard II**

22 Jun–21 Jun

1   1377–8
2   1378–9
3   1379–80
4   1380–1
5   1381–2
6   1382–3
7   1383–4
8   1384–5
9   1385–6
10  1386–7
11  1387–8
12  1388–9
13  1389–90
14  1390–1
15  1391–2
16  1392–3
17  1393–4
18  1394–5
19  1395–6
20  1396–7
21  1397–8
22  1398–99
23  1399–29 Sep 1399

**Henry IV**

30 Sep – 29 Sep

1   1399–1400
2   1400–1
3   1401–2
4   1402–3
5   1403–4
6   1404–5
7   1405–6
8   1406–7
9   1407–8
10  1408–9
11  1409–10
12  1410–1
13  1411–2
14  1412–20 Mar 1413

**Henry V**

21 Mar–20 Mar

1   1413–4
2   1414–5
3   1415–6
4   1416–7
5   1417–8
6   1418–9
7   1419–20
8   1420–1
9   1421–2
10  1422–31 Aug 1422

**Henry VI**

1 Sep–31 Aug

| | |
|---|---|
| 1 | 1422–3 |
| 2 | 1423–4 |
| 3 | 1424–5 |
| 4 | 1425–6 |
| 5 | 1426–7 |
| 6 | 1427–8 |
| 7 | 1428–9 |
| 8 | 1429–30 |
| 9 | 1430–1 |
| 10 | 1431–2 |
| 11 | 1432–3 |
| 12 | 1433–4 |
| 13 | 1434–5 |
| 14 | 1435–6 |
| 15 | 1436–7 |
| 16 | 1437–8 |
| 17 | 1438–9 |
| 18 | 1439–40 |
| 19 | 1440–1 |
| 20 | 1441–2 |
| 21 | 1442–3 |
| 22 | 1443–4 |
| 23 | 1444–5 |
| 24 | 1445–6 |
| 25 | 1446–7 |
| 26 | 1447–8 |
| 27 | 1448–9 |
| 28 | 1449–50 |
| 29 | 1450–1 |
| 30 | 1451–2 |
| 31 | 1452–3 |
| 32 | 1453–4 |
| 33 | 1454–5 |
| 34 | 1455–6 |
| 35 | 1456–7 |
| 36 | 1457–8 |
| 37 | 1458–9 |
| 38 | 1459–60 |
| 39 | 1460–4 Mar 1461 |
| and | |
| 49 | Sep/Oct 1470-11 Apr 1471: Edward IV fled the country on 29 Sep 1740; Henry VI was released on 3 Oct and recrowned on 13 Oct, but was captured by Edward IV on 11 Apr 1741 and the restoration ended. |

**Edward IV**

4 Mar– 3 Mar

| | |
|---|---|
| 1 | 1461–2 |
| 2 | 1462–3 |
| 3 | 1463–4 |
| 4 | 1464–5 |
| 5 | 1465–6 |
| 6 | 1466–7 |
| 7 | 1467–8 |
| 8 | 1468–9 |
| 9 | 1469–70 |

| | | | | | |
|---|---|---|---|---|---|
| 10 | 1470–1 | | 3 | 1487–8 |
| 11 | 1471–2 | | 4 | 1488–9 |
| 12 | 1472–3 | | 5 | 1489–90 |
| 13 | 1473–4 | | 6 | 1490–1 |
| 14 | 1474–5 | | 7 | 1491–2 |
| 15 | 1475–6 | | 8 | 1492–3 |
| 16 | 1476–7 | | 9 | 1493–4 |
| 17 | 1477–8 | | 10 | 1494–5 |
| 18 | 1478–9 | | 11 | 1495–6 |
| 19 | 1479–80 | | 12 | 1496–7 |
| 20 | 1480–1 | | 13 | 1497–8 |
| 21 | 1481–2 | | 14 | 1498–99 |
| 22 | 1482–3 | | 15 | 1499–1500 |
| 23 | 1483–9 Apr 1483 | | 16 | 1500–1 |
| | | | 17 | 1501–2 |
| | | | 18 | 1502–3 |

**Edward V**

19   1503–4

1   9 Apr 1483–25 Jun 1483

20   1504–5
21   1505–6
22   1506–7

**Richard III**

23   1507–8

26 Jun–25 Jun

24   1508– 21 Apr 1509

1   1483–4
2   1484–5

**Henry VIII**

3   1485– 22 Aug 1485

22 Apr–21 Apr

1   1509–10

**Henry VII**

2   1510–1
3   1511–2

22 Aug–21 Aug

4   1512–3
5   1513–4

1   1485–6
2   1486–7

6   1514–5

| | |
|---|---|
| 7 | 1515–6 |
| 8 | 1516–7 |
| 9 | 1517–8 |
| 10 | 1518–9 |
| 11 | 1519–20 |
| 12 | 1520–1 |
| 13 | 1521–2 |
| 14 | 1522–3 |
| 15 | 1523–4 |
| 16 | 1524–5 |
| 17 | 1525–6 |
| 18 | 1526–7 |
| 19 | 1527–8 |
| 20 | 1528–9 |
| 21 | 1529–30 |
| 22 | 1530–1 |
| 23 | 1531–2 |
| 24 | 1532–3 |
| 25 | 1533–4 |
| 26 | 1534–5 |
| 27 | 1535–6 |
| 28 | 1536–7 |
| 29 | 1537–8 |
| 30 | 1538–9 |
| 31 | 1539–40 |
| 32 | 1540–1 |
| 33 | 1541–2 |
| 34 | 1542–3 |
| 35 | 1543–4 |
| 36 | 1544–5 |
| 37 | 1545–6 |
| 38 | 1546– 28 Jan 1547 |

**Edward VI**

28 Jan – 27 Jan

| | |
|---|---|
| 1 | 1547–8 |
| 2 | 1548–9 |
| 3 | 1549–50 |
| 4 | 1550–1 |
| 5 | 1551–2 |
| 6 | 1552–3 |
| 7 | 1553–6 Jul 1553 |

**Jane**

| | |
|---|---|
| 1 | 6 Jul 1553–19 Jul 1553 |

**Mary**

| | |
|---|---|
| 1 | 19 Jul 1553–5 Jul 1554 |
| 2 | 6 Jul 1554–24 Jul 1554 |

**Philip and Mary**

Because Mary dated her second year from 6 Jul (pretending that Jane hadn't existed), her regnal dates with Philip are more complicated – her years partly overlap with his, so his first year equates to part of her second year 2 and part of her third year.

| | | | | |
|---|---|---|---|---|
| 1&2 | 25 Jul 1554–5 Jul 1555 | | 17 | 1574–5 |
| 1&3 | 6 Jul 1555–24 Jul 1555 | | 18 | 1575–6 |
| 2&3 | 25 Jul 1555–5 Jul 1556 | | 19 | 1576–7 |
| 2&4 | 6 Jul 1556–24 Jul 1556 | | 20 | 1577–8 |
| 3&4 | 25 Jul 1556–5 Jul 1557 | | 21 | 1578–9 |
| 3&5 | 6 Jul 1557–24 Jul 1557 | | 22 | 1579–80 |
| 4&5 | 25 Jul 1557–5 Jul 1558 | | 23 | 1580–1 |
| 4&6 | 6 Jul 1558–24 Jul 1558 | | 24 | 1581–2 |
| 5&6 | 25 Jul 1558–17 Nov 1558 | | 25 | 1582–3 |
| | | | 26 | 1583–4 |

**Elizabeth I**

17 Nov–16 Nov

| | | | | |
|---|---|---|---|---|
| 1 | 1558–9 | | 27 | 1584–5 |
| 2 | 1559–60 | | 28 | 1585–6 |
| 3 | 1560–1 | | 29 | 1586–7 |
| 4 | 1561–2 | | 30 | 1587–8 |
| 5 | 1562–3 | | 31 | 1588–9 |
| 6 | 1563–4 | | 32 | 1589–90 |
| 7 | 1564–5 | | 33 | 1590–1 |
| 8 | 1565–6 | | 34 | 1591–2 |
| 9 | 1566–7 | | 35 | 1592–3 |
| 10 | 1567–8 | | 36 | 1593–4 |
| 11 | 1568–9 | | 37 | 1594–5 |
| 12 | 1569–70 | | 38 | 1595–6 |
| 13 | 1570–1 | | 39 | 1596–7 |
| 14 | 1571–2 | | 40 | 1597–8 |
| 15 | 1572–3 | | 41 | 1598–9 |
| 16 | 1573–4 | | 42 | 1599–1600 |
| | | | 43 | 1600–1 |
| | | | 44 | 1601–2 |
| | | | 45 | 1602–24 Mar 1603 |

**James I**

24 Mar–23 Mar

| | |
|---|---|
| 1 | 1603–4 |
| 2 | 1604–5 |
| 3 | 1605–6 |
| 4 | 1606–7 |
| 5 | 1607–8 |
| 6 | 1608–9 |
| 7 | 1609–10 |
| 8 | 1610–1 |
| 9 | 1611–2 |
| 10 | 1612–3 |
| 11 | 1613–4 |
| 12 | 1614–5 |
| 13 | 1615–6 |
| 14 | 1616–7 |
| 15 | 1617–8 |
| 16 | 1618–9 |
| 17 | 1619–20 |
| 18 | 1620–1 |
| 19 | 1621–2 |
| 20 | 1622–3 |
| 21 | 1623–4 |
| 22 | 1624–5 |
| 23 | 1625–27 Mar 1625 |

**Charles I**

27 Mar–26 Mar

| | |
|---|---|
| 1 | 1625–6 |
| 2 | 1626–7 |
| 3 | 1627–8 |
| 4 | 1628–9 |
| 5 | 1629–30 |
| 6 | 1630–1 |
| 7 | 1631–2 |
| 8 | 1632–3 |
| 9 | 1633–4 |
| 10 | 1634–5 |
| 11 | 1635–6 |
| 12 | 1636–7 |
| 13 | 1637–8 |
| 14 | 1638–9 |
| 15 | 1639–40 |
| 16 | 1640–1 |
| 17 | 1641–2 |
| 18 | 1642–3 |
| 19 | 1643–4 |
| 20 | 1644–5 |
| 21 | 1645–6 |
| 22 | 1646–7 |
| 23 | 1647–8 |
| 24 | 1648–30 Jan 1649 |

## Commonwealth

After Charles I's execution on 30
Jan 1649, the Council of State was
set up to govern from 14 Feb 1649
and the monarchy was abolished
on 17 Mar 1649. Cromwell
became the Lord Protector from
16 Dec 1653 until his death on
3 Sep 1658. Cromwell's son
Richard became the Lord
Protector on 3 Sep 1658 and
abdicated on 24 May 1659. The
monarchy was restored when
Charles II was proclaimed king on
5 May 1660; he returned to
England on 29 May 1660.

## Charles II

His regnal years are calculated
from the date of his father's death,
so his first year (year 12) is 29
May 1660 to 29 Jan 1661;
thereafter the dates run from
30 Jan to 29 Jan.

| | |
|---|---|
| 13 | 1661–2 |
| 14 | 1662–3 |
| 15 | 1663–4 |
| 16 | 1664–5 |
| 17 | 1665–6 |
| 18 | 1666–7 |
| 19 | 1667–8 |
| 20 | 1668–9 |
| 21 | 1669–70 |
| 22 | 1670–1 |
| 23 | 1671–2 |
| 24 | 1672–3 |
| 25 | 1673–4 |
| 26 | 1674–5 |
| 27 | 1675–6 |
| 28 | 1676–7 |
| 29 | 1677–8 |
| 30 | 1678–9 |
| 31 | 1679–80 |
| 32 | 1680–1 |
| 33 | 1681–2 |
| 34 | 1682–3 |
| 35 | 1683–4 |
| 36 | 1684–5 |
| 37 | 1685– 6 Feb 1685 |

## James II

6 Feb–5 Feb

| | |
|---|---|
| 1 | 1685–6 |
| 2 | 1686–7 |
| 3 | 1687–8 |
| 4 | 1688 – 11 Dec 1688 |

## Interregnum

12 Dec 1688 – 12 Feb 1689

**William and Mary**

13 Feb – 12 Feb

| | |
|---|---|
| 1 | 1689–90 |
| 2 | 1690–1 |
| 3 | 1691–2 |
| 4 | 1692–3 |
| 5 | 1693–4 |
| 6 | 1694– 27 Dec 1694 |

**William III**

Continued year 6 as 28 Dec 1694–12 Feb 1695; thereafter 13 Feb–12 Feb

| | |
|---|---|
| 7 | 1695–6 |
| 8 | 1696–7 |
| 9 | 1697–8 |
| 10 | 1698–9 |
| 11 | 1699–1700 |
| 12 | 1700–1 |
| 13 | 1701–2 |
| 14 | 1702– 8 Mar 1702 |

**Anne**

8 Mar–7 Mar

| | |
|---|---|
| 1 | 1702–3 |
| 2 | 1703–4 |
| 3 | 1704–5 |
| 4 | 1705–6 |
| 5 | 1706–7 |
| 6 | 1707–8 |
| 7 | 1708–9 |
| 8 | 1709–10 |
| 9 | 1710–1 |
| 10 | 1711–2 |
| 11 | 1712–3 |
| 12 | 1713–4 |
| 13 | 1714–1 Aug 1714 |

**George I**

1 Aug – 31 Jul

| | |
|---|---|
| 1 | 1714–5 |
| 2 | 1715- 6 |
| 3 | 1716–7 |
| 4 | 1717–8 |
| 5 | 1718–9 |
| 6 | 1719–20 |
| 7 | 1720–1 |
| 8 | 1721–2 |
| 9 | 1722–3 |
| 10 | 1723–4 |
| 11 | 1724–5 |
| 12 | 1725–6 |
| 13 | 1726–11 Jun 1727 |

**George II**

11 Jun – 10 Jun from 1727–52; in Sep 1752 the calendar was changed and 11 days were omitted

(see Chapter 2, page 22 for details), so the regnal year of 1752–3 ended on 21 Jun to keep it 365 days in length. From 1753 onwards the regnal year was 22 Jun–21 Jun.

| | |
|---|---|
| 1 | 1727–8 |
| 2 | 1728–9 |
| 3 | 1729–30 |
| 4 | 1730–1 |
| 5 | 1731–2 |
| 6 | 1732–3 |
| 7 | 1733–4 |
| 8 | 1734–5 |
| 9 | 1735–6 |
| 10 | 1736–7 |
| 11 | 1737–8 |
| 12 | 1738–9 |
| 13 | 1739–40 |
| 14 | 1740–1 |
| 15 | 1741–2 |
| 16 | 1742–3 |
| 17 | 1743–4 |
| 18 | 1744–5 |
| 19 | 1745–6 |
| 20 | 1746–7 |
| 21 | 1747–8 |
| 22 | 1748–9 |
| 23 | 1749–50 |
| 24 | 1750–1 |
| 25 | 1751–2 |
| 26 | 1752–3 |
| 27 | 1753–4 |
| 28 | 1754–5 |
| 29 | 1755–6 |
| 30 | 1756–7 |
| 31 | 1757–8 |
| 32 | 1758–9 |
| 33 | 1759–60 |
| 34 | 1760–25 Oct 1760 |

## George III

25 Oct –24 Oct

| | |
|---|---|
| 1 | 1760–1 |
| 2 | 1761–2 |
| 3 | 1762–3 |
| 4 | 1763–4 |
| 5 | 1764–5 |
| 6 | 1765–6 |
| 7 | 1766–7 |
| 8 | 1767–8 |
| 9 | 1768–9 |
| 10 | 1769–70 |
| 11 | 1770–1 |
| 12 | 1771–2 |
| 13 | 1772–3 |
| 14 | 1773–4 |
| 15 | 1774–5 |
| 16 | 1775–6 |
| 17 | 1776–7 |
| 18 | 1777–8 |

| 19 | 1778–9 |
|----|--------|
| 20 | 1779–80 |
| 21 | 1780–1 |
| 22 | 1781–2 |
| 23 | 1782–3 |
| 24 | 1783–4 |
| 25 | 1784–5 |
| 26 | 1785–6 |
| 27 | 1786–7 |
| 28 | 1787–8 |
| 29 | 1788–9 |
| 30 | 1789–90 |
| 31 | 1790–1 |
| 32 | 1791–2 |
| 33 | 1792–3 |
| 34 | 1793–4 |
| 35 | 1794–5 |
| 36 | 1795–6 |
| 37 | 1796–7 |
| 38 | 1797–8 |
| 39 | 1798–9 |
| 40 | 1799–1800 |
| 41 | 1800–1 |
| 42 | 1801–2 |
| 43 | 1802–3 |
| 44 | 1803–4 |
| 45 | 1804–5 |
| 46 | 1805–6 |
| 47 | 1806–7 |
| 48 | 1807–8 |

| 49 | 1808–9 |
|----|--------|
| 50 | 1809–10 |
| 51 | 1810–11 (Regency began 6 Feb 1811) |
| 52 | 1811–2 |
| 53 | 1812–3 |
| 54 | 1813–4 |
| 55 | 1814–5 |
| 56 | 1815–6 |
| 57 | 1816–7 |
| 58 | 1817–8 |
| 59 | 1818–9 |
| 60 | 1819–29 Jan 1820 |

**George IV**

29 Jan–28 Jan

| 1 | 1820–1 |
|----|--------|
| 2 | 1821–2 |
| 3 | 1822–3 |
| 4 | 1823–4 |
| 5 | 1824–5 |
| 6 | 1825–6 |
| 7 | 1826–7 |
| 8 | 1827–8 |
| 9 | 1828–9 |
| 10 | 1829–30 |
| 11 | 1830–26 Jun 1830 |

## William IV

26 Jun–25 Jun

| | |
|---|---|
| 1 | 1830–1 |
| 2 | 1831–2 |
| 3 | 1832–3 |
| 4 | 1833–4 |
| 5 | 1834–5 |
| 6 | 1835–6 |
| 7 | 1836– 20 Jun 1837 |

## Victoria

20 Jun–19 Jun

| | |
|---|---|
| 1 | 1837–8 |
| 2 | 1838–9 |
| 3 | 1839–40 |
| 4 | 1840–1 |
| 5 | 1841–2 |
| 6 | 1842–3 |
| 7 | 1843–4 |
| 8 | 1844–5 |
| 9 | 1845–6 |
| 10 | 1846–7 |
| 11 | 1847–8 |
| 12 | 1848–9 |
| 13 | 1849–50 |
| 14 | 1850–1 |
| 15 | 1851–2 |
| 16 | 1852–3 |
| 17 | 1853–4 |
| 18 | 1854–5 |
| 19 | 1855–6 |
| 20 | 1856–7 |
| 21 | 1857–8 |
| 22 | 1858–9 |
| 23 | 1859–60 |
| 24 | 1860–1 |
| 25 | 1861–2 |
| 26 | 1862–3 |
| 27 | 1863–4 |
| 28 | 1864–5 |
| 29 | 1865–6 |
| 30 | 1866–7 |
| 31 | 1867–8 |
| 32 | 1868–9 |
| 33 | 1869–70 |
| 34 | 1870–1 |
| 35 | 1871–2 |
| 36 | 1872–3 |
| 37 | 1873–4 |
| 38 | 1874–5 |
| 39 | 1875–6 |
| 40 | 1876–7 |
| 41 | 1877–8 |
| 42 | 1878–9 |
| 43 | 1879–80 |
| 44 | 1880–1 |
| 45 | 1881–2 |
| 46 | 1882–3 |
| 47 | 1883–4 |
| 48 | 1884–5 |
| 49 | 1885–6 |

| | |
|---|---|
| 50 | 1886–7 |
| 51 | 1887–8 |
| 52 | 1888–9 |
| 53 | 1889–90 |
| 54 | 1890–1 |
| 55 | 1891–2 |
| 56 | 1892–3 |
| 57 | 1893–4 |
| 58 | 1894–5 |
| 59 | 1895–6 |
| 60 | 1896–7 |
| 61 | 1897–8 |
| 62 | 1898–9 |
| 63 | 1899–1900 |
| 64 | 1900–22 Jan 1901 |

**Edward VII**

22 Jan–21 Jan

| | |
|---|---|
| 1 | 1901–2 |
| 2 | 1902–3 |
| 3 | 1903–4 |
| 4 | 1904–5 |
| 5 | 1905–6 |
| 6 | 1906–7 |
| 7 | 1907–8 |
| 8 | 1908–9 |
| 9 | 1909–10 |
| 10 | 1910– 6 May 1910 |

**George V**

6 May–5 May

| | |
|---|---|
| 1 | 1910–1 |
| 2 | 1911–2 |
| 3 | 1912–3 |
| 4 | 1913–4 |
| 5 | 1914–5 |
| 6 | 1915–6 |
| 7 | 1916–7 |
| 8 | 1917–8 |
| 9 | 1918–9 |
| 10 | 1919–20 |
| 11 | 1920–1 |
| 12 | 1921–2 |
| 13 | 1922–3 |
| 14 | 1923–4 |
| 15 | 1924–5 |
| 16 | 1925–6 |
| 17 | 1926–7 |
| 18 | 1927–8 |
| 19 | 1928–9 |
| 20 | 1929–30 |
| 21 | 1930–1 |
| 22 | 1931–2 |
| 23 | 1932–3 |
| 24 | 1933–4 |
| 25 | 1934–5 |
| 26 | 1935– 20 Jan 1936 |

**Edward VIII**

22 Jan–21 Jan

1   20 Jan 1901 – 11 Dec 1936

**George VI**

11 Dec–10 Dec

1   1936–7
2   1937–8
3   1938–9
4   1939–40

5   1940–1
6   1941–2
7   1942–3
8   1943–4
9   1944–5
10   1945–6
11   1946–7
12   1947–8
13   1948–9
14   1949–50
15   1950–1
16   1951– 6 Feb 1952

## ROMAN DATES

Some documents use Roman dates, i.e. so many days before or after the Kalends, Nones or Ides. The Kalends were always the 1st of the month; the Ides and Nones differed slightly.

| Month | Nones | Ides |
|---|---|---|
| January | 5 | 13 |
| February | 5 | 13 |
| March | 7 | 15 |
| April | 5 | 13 |
| May | 7 | 15 |
| June | 5 | 13 |
| July | 7 | 15 |
| August | 5 | 13 |
| September | 5 | 13 |
| October | 7 | 15 |
| November | 5 | 13 |
| December | 5 | 13 |

However, there are a couple of oddities.

Firstly, when you counted the number of days, you included the referenced day itself. So:

- The Ides of March – 15
- The day before the Ides of March (pridie Idus) is 14 March
- The third day before the Ides of March is 13 March (not the 12th – because you include the Ides as the first day).

Secondly, in a leap year, the Romans put 29 days in February by adding an extra 6th day before the Kalends of March. So:

- the 6th day before the Kalends of March is 25 February
- the second 6th day before the Kalends of March is 24 February

## QUARTER DAYS
Lady Day – 25 March
Midsummer – 24 June
Michaelmas – 29 September
Christmas – 25 December

## LAW TERMS
You may see some documents dated with the form of law term followed by regnal year; this is most likely to be on parliamentary bills and acts, legal papers, final concords and common recoveries. Law terms evolved because cases had to be suspended at certain times of the year, when legal business could not be conducted.

- Michaelmas – 1 October to 21 December
- Hilary – 11 January to the Wednesday before Easter Saturday

- Easter – the 2nd Tuesday after Easter Sunday to the Friday before Whit Sunday
- Trinity – the 2nd Tuesday after Whit Sunday to 31 July.

# Appendix 5

# List of County Record Offices

**Bedfordshire**
Bedfordshire and Luton Archives
and Records Service
Riverside Building
County Hall
Bedford
MK42 9AP
Tel: 01234 228833
Website:www.bedfordshire.gov.uk/
archive

**Berkshire**
Berkshire Record Office
9 Coley Avenue
Reading
RG1 6AF
Tel: 0118 901 5132
Website: www.berkshirerecord
office.org.uk

**Buckinghamshire**
Centre for Buckinghamshire
Studies (houses former
Buckinghamshire Record Office)
County Hall
Walton Street
Aylesbury
HP20 1UU
Tel: 01296 382587 (archives)
(01296) 382250 (local studies)
Website: www.buckscc.gov.uk/
archives

**Cambridgeshire**
Cambridgeshire County Record
Office
Shire Hall
Castle Hill
Cambridge
CB3 0AP
Tel: 01223 717281
Website: www.cambridgeshire.
gov.uk/leisure/archives

**Cheshire**

Cheshire & Chester Archives and
Local Studies Service
Cheshire Record Office
Duke Street
Chester
CH1 1RL
Tel: 01244 602574
Website: www.cheshire.gov.uk/
recoff/home.htm

**Cleveland**

Teesside Archives
Exchange House
Exchange Square
Middlesbrough
TS1 1DB
Tel: 01642 248321
Website: www.middlesbrough.
gov.uk/ccm/navigation/
leisure-and-culture/archives/

**Cornwall**

Cornwall Record Office
Old County Hall
Treyew Road
Truro
TR1 3AY
Tel: 01872 323127
Website: www.cornwall.gov.uk/
index.cfm?articleid=307

**Cumbria**

Cumbria Record Office
The Castle
Carlisle
CA3 8UR
Tel: 01228 607285
Website: www.cumbria.gov.uk/
archives/recordoffices.carec.asp

**Derbyshire**

Derbyshire Record Office
County Hall
Matlock
Derbyshire
DE4 3AG
Tel: 01629 585347
Website: www.derbyshire.gov.uk/
leisure/record_office/

**Devon**

Devon Record Office
Great Moor House
Bittern Road
Sowton
Exeter
EX2 7NL
Tel: 01392 384253
Website: www.devon.gov.uk/
record_office.htm

**Dorset**

Dorset History Centre (formerly
Dorset Record Office)
Bridport Road
Dorchester
Dorset
DR1 1RP
Tel: 01305 250550
Website: www.dorsetforyou.com/
index.jsp?articleid=2203

**Durham**

Durham County Record Office
County Hall
Durham
DH1 5UL
Tel: 0191 383 3253
Website:
www.durham.gov.uk/recordoffice

**Essex**

Essex Record Office
Wharf Road
Chelmsford
Essex
CM2 6YT
Tel: 01245 244644
Website: www.essexcc.gov.uk/ero

**Gloucestershire**

Gloucestershire Record Office
Clarence Row
Alvin Street
Gloucester
GL1 3DW
Tel: 01452 425295
Website: www.gloucestershire.
gov.uk/index.cfm?articleid=1348

**Hampshire**

Hampshire Record Office
Sussex Street
Winchester
SO23 8TH
Tel: 01962 846154
Website: www.hants.gov.uk/
record-office

**Herefordshire**

Herefordshire Record Office
Harold Street
Hereford
HR1 2QX
Tel: 01432 260750
Website:
www.herefordshire.gov.uk/archive
s/3584.asp

**Kent**
Centre for Kentish Studies
Sessions House
County Hall
Maidstone
ME4 1XQ
Tel: 01622 694363
Website: www.kent.gov.uk/
leisure-and-culture/archives-and-
local-history/

**Lancashire**
Lancashire Record Office
Bow Lane
Preston
Lancashire
PR1 2RE
Tel: 01772 533039
Website:
www.lancashire.gov.uk/educa-
tion/record_office/

**Leicestershire**
The Record Office for
Leicestershire, Leicester and
Rutland
Long Street
Wigston Magna
Leicester
LE18 2AH
Tel: 0116 257 1080
Website: http://www.leics.gov.uk/
index/community/museums/record
_office.htm

**London**
London Metropolitan Archives
40 Northampton Road
London
EC1R 0HB
Tel: 020 7332 3820
Website: www.cityoflondon.gov.uk/
Corporation/leisure_heritage/
libraries_archives_museums_
galleries/lma/lma.htm

**Manchester (Lancashire and
Cheshire)**
Greater Manchester County
Record Office
56 Marshall Street
New Cross
Manchester M4 5FU
Tel: 0161 832 5284
Website: www.gmcro.co.uk

**Merseyside**
Liverpool Record Office
Central Library
William Brown Street
Liverpool L3 8EW
Tel: 0151 233 5817
Website:
www.liverpool.gov.uk/Leisure_
and_culture/Local_history_and_
heritage/index.asp

**Norfolk**
Norfolk Record Office
The Archive Centre
Martineau Lane
Norwich
NR1 2DQ
Tel: 01603 222599
Website:
www.archives.norfolk.gov.uk

**Northamptonshire**
Northamptonshire Record Office
Wootton Hall Park
Northampton
NN4 9BQ
Tel: 01604 762129
Website: www.northamptonshire.
gov.uk/Community/record/about_
us.htm

**Northumberland**
Northumberland Collections
Service
Woodhorn
Queen Elizabeth II Country Park
Ashington
Northumberland
NR63 9YF
Tel: 01670 528080
Website: www.northumberland.
gov.uk/collections

**Nottinghamshire**
Nottinghamshire Archives
County House
Castle Meadow Road
Nottingham
NG2 1AG
Tel: 0115 958 1634
Website: www.nottinghamshire.
gov.uk/archives

**Oxfordshire**
Oxfordshire Record Office
St Luke's Church
Temple Road
Cowley
Oxford
OX4 2HT
Tel: 01865 398200
Website: www.oxfordshire.gov.uk

**Shropshire**
Shropshire Archives
Castle Gates
Shrewsbury
SY1 2AQ
Tel: 01743 255350
Website: www.shropshire.gov.uk/
archives.nsf

**Somerset**
Somerset Archives and Record
Service
Obridge Road
Taunton
TA2 7PU
Tel: 01823 278805
Website: www.somerset.gov
.uk/archives

**Staffordshire**
Staffordshire Record Office
Eastgate Street
Stafford
ST16 2LZ
Tel: 01785 278379
Website: www.staffordshire.
gov.uk/archives

**Suffolk**
Suffolk Record Office
Gatacre Road
Ipswich
IP1 2LQ
Tel: 01473 584541
Website: www.suffolkcc.gov.uk/sro/

**Sussex**
East Sussex Record Office
The Maltings
Castle Precincts
Lewes
BN7 1YT
Tel: 01273 482349
Website: www.eastsussex.gov.uk/
leisureandtourism/localandfamily-
hisotry.scro

West Sussex Record Office
3 Orchard Street
Chichester
PO19 1RN
Tel: 01243 753602
Website:
www.westsussex.gov.uk/ccm/
navigation/libraries-and-
archives/record-office/

**Tyne and Wear**
Tyne and Wear Archive Service
Blandford House
Blandford Square
Newcastle upon Tyne
NE1 4JA
Tel: 0191 277 2248
Website: www.tyneandwear
archives.org.uk

**Warwickshire**
Warwickshire County Record
Office
Priory Park
Cape Road
Warwick
CV34 4JS
Tel: 01926 738959
Website: www.warwickshire.
gov.uk/web/corporate/pages/links/
DEEC2ES9DB9499B780256A33
0054CA30

**Wiltshire**
Wiltshire and Swindon Record
Office
Libraries and Heritage HQ
Wiltshire County Council
Bythesea Road
Trowbridge
BA14 8BS
Tel: 01225 713138
Website: www.wiltshire.gov.uk/
archives

**Worcestershire**
Worcestershire Record Office
County Hall
Spetchley Road
Worcester WR5 2NP
Tel: 01905 766351
Website: www.worcestershire.
whub.org.uk/home/wccindex/
wcc-records.htm

**Yorkshire**
North Yorkshire County Record
Office
Malpas Road
Northallerton
DL7 8TB
Tel: 01609 777585
Website:
www.northyorks.gov.uk/public/
site?NYCC/menuitem.0329f0efd5
84164fd7428f1040008a0c/?vgn

**East Riding of Yorkshire
Archives and Local Studies**
The Treasure House
Champney Road
Beverley
Tel: 01482 392790
Website:
www.eastriding.gov.uk/libraries/
archives/index.html

**West Yorkshire Archive Service**
Newstead Road
Wakefield
WF1 2DE
Tel: 01924 305980
Website: www.archives.wyjs.org.uk/

# Appendix 6

# Glossary of Terms

This section contains a glossary of common terms found in records. Anything in *italics* means that the term has its own glossary entry with more details.

**abstract of title** shows how the title to the land passed to the current owner – a summary of previous deeds that are not included with the title deeds (e.g. if the original deeds involved several properties which were sold to different owners, each new owner would have had an abstract of title rather than the original deeds).

**abuttal** in title deeds, this refers to the names of the owners or tenants of adjoining properties.

**advowson** the right to nominate someone to an ecclesiastical *benefice,* held by a patron who presents the candidate to the bishop (candidate may be refused and can buy, sell or give away an advowson).

**alienate** to transfer land to someone else.

**almanac** the annual calendar of months and days usually containing astronomical data, weather, and similar information.

**almoner** a monk responsible for collecting and distributing alms.

**amercement** a fine levied by a court.

**appurtenances** other things belonging to lands such as gardens and orchards, also rights attached to a piece of land.

**assignment** the transfer of right.

**assize** a legal procedure (i.e. court where circuit judges presided ); may also refer to measures, e.g. 'assize of bread' was the local government's measure of the quality and price of bread.

**bailiff** responsible for day-to-day management of the manor, for a salary (see also *reeve*).

**banns** the public announcement of an intended marriage, often read aloud in church for three successive Sundays before a marriage.

**benefice** an ecclesiastical office (i.e. that of dean, rector, perpetual curate, vicar) where the person holding the office is referred to as an *incumbent*.

**bill of complaint** a petition addressed to the lord chancellor and the first pleadings in a case.

**bundle** in an archive, this is a collection of documents tied together.

**calendar** a list of documents (such as details of prisoners), usually arranged in date order.

**capital messuage** a high-status house such as a manor house occupied by the owner of land containing several *messuages*.

**cartulary** a book with copies of deeds, charters and legal records (often monastic).

**cellarer** the monk responsible for food supplies and trading outside of an instutution.

**chattels** personal property (portable).

**churchwarden** an elected representative of the *parish* (there were usually two: one elected by the *incumbent* and one by the parishioners).

**closure period** the time during which documents are held in an archive but are not available to the public to access for legal or privacy reasons.

**codicil** the supplement to a will.

**constable** the keeper of law and order, appointed by the jury of the *leet court*; after the decline of manors, the constable was appointed annually at the parish vestry meeting. The post was unpaid and had no expenses.

**contumacy** a wilful refusal to comply with the summons or order of the court.

**conveyance** the transfer of freehold land from one party to another.

**copyhold** the land belonging the the manor. Customary tenants held a 'copy' of the entry in the manor court roll which recorded them as tenants. After the Law of Property Act 1922 all copyhold land was converted to freehold.

**court roll** a record of the *manorial court's* business transaction (originally the parchment was filed as a roll, but even when books were used they were still referred to as 'rolls').

**covenant** an agreement in a deed between two parties. A restrictive covenant means an agreement not to do something (e.g. digging up bricks, keeping pigs, extending a house beyond the building lines, using a house as a pub).

**curtilage** a yard or court attached to a dwelling house and including its outbuildings, seen by the law as forming one enclosure.

**custumal** the inventory of the revenue given by tenants to the lord of the manor.

**demesne** the possession of an estate as your own.

**diocese** the district of a bishop's jurisdiction.

**dower** a widow had the right to $\frac{1}{3}$ of her late husband's property.

**easement** a right without profit (e.g. a *right of way* over land).

**ejectio firmae** a legal action, either by the owner to eject a tenant who refused to leave when the lease had expired, or by a tenant who had been thrown out before the lease had expired.

**electoral roll** the list of people eligible to vote (names and addresses have been listed since 1928).

**enclosure** (also shown as 'inclosure') a process where strips of land in open fields were converted into smaller fields enclosed by hedges or fences and the original owners were given the equivalent of the strips in the new fields. Usually done under Act of Parliament.

**entail** see *fee entail*.

**estreat roll** a court record giving details of *amercements* i.e. lists of names of tenants, their offences and the fine.

**executor** a man who carries out the will of the deceased (a woman is an executrix).

**extent** details of a *demesne* listed in a set order, starts with the manor house and ending with the tenants' rents and services.

**fee entail** an estate bequeathed under a strict order of succession (such as husband to wife, or father to eldest son) that could not be disposed of in any other way; the current owner is the 'tenant for life' and their heir is the 'tenant in tail'.

**fee simple** a freehold and therefore owned absolutely (and so could be bequeathed however the owner liked).

**finding aid** a catalogue or index in an archive to help researchers find what they need.

**frankpledge** a pledge or surety made by freemen in a *tithing*, vouching for the good behaviour of freeborn citizens over the age of 14 and that anyone who broke the law would come to court to answer for it (cases were heard twice a year).

**freehold** the holding of land without having to give service to the manor; freeholders had secure tenure and no restrictions on their right to dispose of their lands. Lands could be held as either *fee simple* or *fee entail*.

**glebe** the landed endowment of a parish church (glebe land could not be sold or exchanged until the 19th century; the *incumbent* didn't own the freehold).

**habendum** part of a deed defining what estate or interest is granted (usually starts with the words 'habendum et tenendum', i.e. 'to have and to hold').

**hereditament** property that can be inherited. A 'corporeal hereditament' has physical form, such as land or houses, and an 'incorporeal hereditament' has a non-physical form, such as a right.

**heriot** the payment due to the lord of the manor at a tenant's death (often a year's rent, the best beast, or the best possession); heriots were abolished by the Copyhold Act 1852 and the Copyhold Act 1858.

**hundred** the administrative division of a county (that usually held several parishes).

**inclosure** see *enclosure*.

**incumbent** a person who holds a *benefice*.

**indenture** an agreement, often written several times on the same parchment (one for each party to the agreement); the copies were separated by an irregular cut to prevent forgery.

**infirmarium** a monk responsible for an infirmary or sick bay.

**intestate** dying without making a legal will.

**knight's fee** a payment to the lord of the manor for *freehold* property, equivalent of the fee to provide a fully armed knight and his servants for 40 days each year; this fee could be divided among several tenants.

**leasehold** land held by a leaseholder (i.e. assigned rather than conveyed).

**leaseholder** a person holding land that has been leased for a specified time (often 21 years).

**ledger** a book in which the accounts of a firm are kept.

**leet court** a manor court authorised to hear cases of petty jurisdiction and the administration of communal agriculture.

**legacy** property transferred by a will.

**letters patent** a document from the sovereign or government conferring a patent or right, written on the Patent Rolls.

**living** a *benefice*, or a position in the church such as a parish.

**manor** a feudal freehold estate (note that they varied in size – there could be several manors in a large parish, or one manor could spread over several parishes).

**manorial court** the court held by the lord of the manor via his steward; any business transacted was written up in the *court rolls*.

**messuage** a dwelling house, along with its grounds and outbuildings (see also *capital messuage*).

**minutes** the summary of proceedings at a meeting.

**nisi prius** the trial of civil cases by a jury.

**obedientary** a monk in charge of administration in a monastery.

**overseer of the poor** appointed by the parish to provide the relief or maintenance of poor people in the parish; levied the parish rate (poor rate) or tax to cover the money paid out. (The office was first set up under the Poor Relief Act 1601.)

**Oyer and Terminer** hearing and giving judgement. (The court of Oyer and Terminer was the final judgement, usually by the king.)

**parish** an administrative area which provided the resources to support a church and maintain its priest.

**petty sessions** the lowest tier in the English court system (known as magistrates' courts in modern times); relate to criminal cases heard by magistrates or Justices of the Peace, but also relate to the licensing of pubs.

**pightle** an enclosed yard or croft (usually next to a dwelling house).

**pipe roll** a record of payments made to the exchequer.

**pittancer** a monk responsible for supplying pittances (extra food given to the community on feast days).

**plea** an action at law, with the court of common pleas hearing civil actions.

**presentment** in *Quarter Sessions* files, a statement of fact from the Justice of the Peace or a constable.

**probate** the process of proving a will (i.e. showing its validity). Before 1858 this was done via church courts. This was written up in the grant of probate.

**quarter sessions** the main judicial bodies of the English counties; met four times a year, and cases were heard by Justices of the Peace. Dealt with criminal affairs until 1971; also dealt with administration (such as apprenticeship, transport, land use) until replaced by county councils in 1889.

**quitclaim** a legal document renouncing any rights to property.

**quitrent** the rent paid to the lord of the manor by *copyhold* tenants in place of military services.

**recognisance** a bond agreed in court binding someone to undertake an action. Usually made at Quarter Sessions but Justices of the Peace could also take recognisances outside the sessions.

**rector** the *incumbent* in a parish, receiving the tithes of parishioners.

**recusant** someone who refuses to attend the established church (the legal offence is known as recusancy).

**reeve** a deputy. The shire reeve was the king's deputy in the county; the manor reeve was the lord of the manor's deputy in the court and his duties were the same as a *bailiff* except he was elected by the tenants rather than paid a salary.

**refectorian** a monk in charge of a refectory and their names.

**regnal year** the current year of a sovereign's reign, counted from the date of accession.

**removal order** made by a Justice of the Peace to send someone back to their parish of origin (usually found on a *settlement certificate*).

**rental roll** records amounts paid by tenants (which might not be the same as the amount they were due to pay) and their names.

**restrictive covenant** – see *covenant*.

**right of way** the right of a specified person to go from point A to point B over the land of another specified person.

**sacrist** the official in charge of items used during religious services (also known as a sacristan or sexton).

**scutage** the payment of money rather than military service to the king.

**secular clergy** priests who live with the general population rather than in a monastic community (e.g. a curate, parish priest, bishop).

**seisin** (or seizin) the possession of *freehold* property.

**seneschal** a steward.

**sequestrate** the confiscation or seizure of goods.

**settlement** in terms of deeds, the transfer of properties to trustees for a particular purpose (e.g. a marriage settlement is usually made before a marriage; a family settlement involves property held for the spouse and children, i.e. setting up an *entail*).

**settlement certificate** issued by the parish to someone who moved to another parish. If, under the Poor Law, the person had to be maintained by the parish, the authorities would ask about their settlement and could make a *removal order* to send them back to their parish of origin.

**spiritualities** tithes, gifts and ecclesiastical income belonging to a bishop or religious house. (See also *temporalities.*)

**survey** in manorial documents, the detailed description of a manor – the boundaries, the customs and the rent roll/rental, giving the names of tenants and details of their land, tenure and the rent paid.

**synod** a church council or assembly.

**temporalities** the land, buildings and secular income belonging to a bishop or religious house. (See also spiritualities.)

**tenement** property, usually buildings; a *messuage* may contain one tenement or may be divided into several tenements.

**tenure** form of right by which someone holds property (see *copyhold, freehold, leasehold*).

**terrier** a register of landed property describing the boundaries and acreage.

**tithe** the payment to the church of $\frac{1}{10}$ th of the produce of the land. Great tithes (main products such as crops) went to the *rector* and small tithes (harder to collect, such as eggs) to the vicar. Over time tithes were paid as a cash equivalent rather than actual produce.

**tithing** a group of householders in the *frankpledge* system (which originally had ten members and a head known as a decener).

**vestry** the room where parish meetings were held between the minister, church wardens and leading parishioners.

**vicar** appointed by an absentee *rector*; received the small *tithes*.

**virgate** an area of land (usually in common fields and often denoting 32 acres, but the amount of land varied in practice).

**visitation** a visit by a bishop or archdeacon to a diocese, parish or religious institution.

# Appendix 7

# Weights and Measures

Weights and measures often crop up in documents, and as many of the names have not been used for years it is worth having a ready guide to hand. This appendix covers:

- Averdupois weight
- Troy weight
- Apothecaries' weight
- Wool weight
- Liquid capacity
- Dry measurement capacity
- Linear measure
- Square measure.

## AVERDUPOIS WEIGHT

Averdupois weight was used to measure large or bulky items and eventually became the standard for most weights.

| 16 drams (or drachms) | 1 ounce (oz) |
| 16 ounces | 1 pound (lb) |
| 14 pounds | 1 stone |
| 28 pounds | 1 quarter |
| 4 quarters | 1 hundredweight (cwt) (= 112 lbs) |
| 20 hundredweight | 1 ton (= 2,240 lbs) |

You may also see references to:

a cental = 100 lbs
a 'short ton' or 'American ton' = 2,000 lbs.

## TROY WEIGHT

Troy weight measured small amounts of precious metal and gemstones. The Troy ounce is still used, but the Troy pound was abolished by the Weights and Measures Act 1878. Note that the Troy pound is a lot lighter than the averdupois pound.

| 24 grains | 1 pennyweight (dwt) |
|---|---|
| 20 pennyweight | 1 ounce (oz) |
| 12 ounces | 1 pound (lb) |

## APOTHECARIES' WEIGHT

This was similar to Troy weight, used for measuring small amounts of powders. Apothecaries' pounds and ounces were the same as Troy pounds and ounces. The measures were abolished by the Weights and Measures Act 1878.

| 20 grains | 1 scruple |
|---|---|
| 3 scruples | 1 drachm (or dram) |
| 8 drams | 1 ounce (oz) |
| 12 ounces | 1 pound (lb) |

## WOOL WEIGHT

There were 240 lbs in a pack of wool, but other measures used included:

| 7 lbs | 1 clove |
|---|---|
| 4 cloves | 1 todd |
| $6\frac{1}{2}$ todds | 1 wey (182 lbs) |
| 2 weys = 1 sack | 1 sack |

## LIQUID CAPACITY

The following covers liquids, but some dry goods were also measured by volume rather than weight – for example, in the 1700s mushrooms were measured by volume.

A corn gallon was used to measure dry goods; it was defined in 1696 as the 'Winchester Measure' and was 268.8 cubic inches.

There were other gallon measures in use – an ale gallon was 282 cubic inches and a wine gallon was 231 cubic inches.

In 1824 all gallon measures were standardised, with effect from 1 January 1826. The new Imperial gallon was 277.42 cubic inches, equivalent to 10 lbs averdupois of distilled water at a temperature of 62 degrees F.

### For liquid measures up to a gallon:

| | |
|---|---|
| 20 minims | 1 fluid scruple |
| 3 fluid scruple | 1 fluid drachm |
| 8 fluid drachm | 1 fluid ounce (fl. oz.) |
| 5 fluid ounces | 1 gill |
| 4 gills (20 fl. oz.) | 1 pint |
| 2 pints | 1 quart |
| 4 quarts | 1 gallon |

### Ale and beer measurements (1688–1803)

| | |
|---|---|
| $8\frac{1}{2}$ gallons | 1 firkin |
| 2 firkins | 1 kilderkin |
| 2 kilderkins | 1 barrel |
| 42 gallons | 1 tierce |
| $1\frac{1}{2}$ barrels (51 gallons) | 1 hogshead |
| 2 barrels (68 gallons) | 1 puncheon |
| 2 hogsheads (102 gallons) | 1 pipe or butt |
| 3 puncheons (204 gallons) | 1 tun |

## Ale and beer measurements (1803 onwards)

| | |
|---|---|
| $4\frac{1}{2}$ gallons | 1 pin |
| 2 pins | 1 firkin |
| 2 firkins | 1 kilderkin |
| 2 kilderkins | 1 barrel |
| $1\frac{1}{2}$ barrels (54 gallons) | 1 hogshead |
| 2 barrels (72 gallons) | 1 puncheon |
| 2 hogsheads (108 gallons) | 1 butt |
| 3 puncheons (216 gallons) | 1 tun |

## Wines, spirits, cider, oil and vinegar measures before 1824

| | |
|---|---|
| 18 gallons | 1 rundlet |
| $31\frac{1}{2}$ gallons | 1 barrel |
| 42 gallons | 1 tierce |
| 2 barrels (63 gallons) | 1 hogshead |
| 2 tierces (84 gallons) | 1 puncheon |
| 2 hogsheads or 3 tierces (126 gallons) | 1 pipe or butt |
| 2 pipes or 3 puncheons (252 gallons) | 1 tun |

## Wines, spirits, cider, oil and vinegar measures after 1824

| | |
|---|---|
| 15 Imperial gallons | 1 rundlet |
| $26\frac{1}{4}$ imperial gallons | 1 barrel |
| 35 Imperial gallons | 1 tierce |
| $3\frac{1}{2}$ rundlets or 2 barrels ($52\frac{1}{2}$ Imperial gallons) | 1 hogshead |
| 2 tierces (70 Imperial gallons) | 1 puncheon |
| 2 hogsheads or 3 tierces (105 Imperial gallons) | 1 pipe or butt |
| 2 pipes (210 Imperial gallons) | 1 tun |

# DRY MEASUREMENT CAPACITY

| 4 gills | 1 pint |
|---|---|
| 2 pints | 1 quart |
| 4 quarts | 1 gallon |
| 2 gallons | 1 peck |
| 4 pecks | 1 bushel |
| 3 bushels | 1 sack or bag (coal) |
| 2 bushels | 1 strike (or raser) |
| 4 bushels | 1 coomb (usually grain) |
| 8 bushels | 1 quarter |
| 5 quarters | 1 load (or wey) |
| 36 bushels (12 sacks) | 1 chaldron (coal) |
| 2 weys (80 bushels) | 1 last |

# LINEAR MEASURE

| 3 barleycorns | 1 inch |
|---|---|
| 4 inches | 1 hand |
| 12 inches | 1 foot |
| 3 feet | 1 yard |
| $5\frac{1}{2}$ yards | 1 pole (may also be called a rod or perch) |
| 4 poles | 1 chain (land surveyor's measure – there were 100 links in a chain) |
| 10 chains | 1 furlong |
| 8 furlongs | 1 mile (1,760 yards) |
| 3 miles | 1 league |

Although a rood is usually a square measure (see below), you may come across it as a unit of length in fencing, hedging and ditching, where it is equivalent to 8 yards.

# SQUARE MEASURE

An acre was originally the amount of land that could be ploughed by a team of eight oxen in one day. A hide was the amount that could support a typical family, ploughed by a team of eight oxen in a year, nominally around 120 acres; another name for a hide was a carucate. There were two oxgangs (or bovates) in a virgate, and four virgates in a hide.

The standard measure of an acre was 660 feet long and 66 feet wide. (One furlong = '1 furrow long'.)

| 144 square inches | 1 square foot |
|---|---|
| 9 square feet | 1 square yard |
| $30\frac{1}{4}$ square yards | 1 perch (may also be called a rod or pole) |
| 40 perches | 1 rood |
| 4 roods | 1 acre |
| 640 acres | 1 square mile |

# Index